MARRIED IN 1975

Elizabeth Absalom & MALCOLM WATSON

D'AZUR PUBLISHING

Published by D'Azur Publishing 2025
D'Azur Publishing is a Division of D'Azur Limited

Copyright © D'Azur Publishing 2025
Elizabeth Absalom and Malcolm Watson have asserted her right under the Copyright, Design and Patents Act 1988 to be identified as the authors of this work.

The language, phrases and terminology within this book are as written at the time of the news reports during the year covered and convey and illustrate the sentiments at that time, even though modern society may find some words inappropriate. The news reports are taken from internationally recognised major newspapers and other sources of the year in question. The language does not represent any personal view of the author or publisher.

All Rights Reserved. No part of this publication may be reproduced, stored or transmitted in any form or by any means, electronic, mechanical, digital or otherwise, except under the terms of the Copyright, Designs and Patents Act 1988 or under terms of a licence issued by the publisher. This book is sold subject to the condition that it shall not, by way of trade or otherwise, be lent, resold or hired out, or otherwise circulated without the publishers prior consent in any form or binding or cover other than that in which it is published and without a similar condition, including this condition, being imposed on the subsequent purchaser. All requests to the Publisher for permission should be addressed to info@d-azur.com.

First published in Great Britain in 2025 by D'Azur Limited
Contact: info@d-azur.com Visit www.d-azur.com

ISBN 9798306559339

ACKNOWLEDGEMENTS
The publisher wishes to acknowledge the following people and sources:

British Newspaper Archive; The Times Archive; Cover Malcolm Watson; p7 (Railway Engine) Malcolm Watson; p12 Apple Computer Binarysequence; p19 (Liberty's Facade) Jon; p19 (Liberty's Sign) James G; p49 (Evacuation) Hubert van Es; p65 (Ashe) Bogaerts, Rob; p67 (Bag Piper) K. Mitch Hodge; p67 (showground) RHASS; p67 (dancing) Stirling Highland Games; p77 (sculpture) Tony Hisgett ; p83 Edinburgh Fringe Festival; p85 (Main) Zekia Salmon-Hall; p103 (main) The Watercress Line; p107 (Main) Véronique H;

Whilst we have made every effort to contact copyright holders, should we have made any omission, please contact us so that we can make the appropriate acknowledgement.

CONTENTS

1975 Highlights Of The Year　　　　　4-5

1975 The Year You Were Married　　　6-7

1975 Sporting Events　　　　　　　　8-9

1975 Cultural Events　　　　　　　　10-11

1975 Science and Nature　　　　　　14-15

1975 Lives Of Everyday People　　　16-17

THE YEAR DAY-BY-DAY　　　　　　**18-119**

The 1975 calendar　　　　　　　　　120

1975 Highlights

Monarch: Queen Elizabeth II   Prime Minister: Ted Heath (Conservative) From March 4th Harold Wilson (Labour)

In 1975 the Sex Discrimination and Equal Pay Acts paved the way for a fairer society. Bill Gates founded Microsoft at the age of 19, and Margaret Thatcher became the first woman leader of the Conservative party.

The weather was equally astonishing with snow showers as far south as London in June. The Sex Pistols made their debut in November establishing Punk Rock on the music scene, while on the TV we watched Fawlty Towers.

In September, Dougal Haston and Doug Scott became the first British climbers to reach the summit of Mount Everest .

The Birmingham Six are wrongfully sentenced to life imprisonment and, Lord Lucan is found guilty of wilful murder of the nanny who was found dead at his wife's home.

Mt. Everest

FAMOUS PEOPLE WHO WERE BORN IN 1975

25th Feb: Naga Munchetty, television presenter
2nd May: David Beckham, footballer
27th May: Jamie Oliver, chef and TV personality
29th May: Melanie Brown, singer and Spice Girls member
4th Jun: Alex Wharf, English cricketer
26th Jul: Liz Truss, politician
5th Oct: Kate Winslet, actress
9th Nov: Gareth Malone, choir master
12th Nov: Katherine Grainger, rower

FAMOUS PEOPLE WHO MARRIED IN 1975

Jan 21st Vsa Zsa Gabor and Jack Ryan
May 6th Sean Connery and Micheline Roquebrune
June 30th Cher and Gregg Allman
Aug 23rd Maggie Smith and Beverley Cross
Sept 20th Dudley Moore and Tuesday Weld
Oct 10th Elizabeth Taylor and Richard Burton
Oct 11th Bill Clinton and Hillary Rodham
Oct 18th Lionel Ritchie and and Brenda Harvey
Oct 17th Maurice Gibb and Yvonne Spencley
Dec 19th Buzz Aldrin and Beverly Van Zile

Of The Year

JANUARY The Beatles partnership is finally dissolved at a High Court hearing, eight years after they debuted and five years after the group split up.

FEBRUARY Margaret Thatcher defeats Edward Heath in the Conservative Party leadership election, becoming the party's first woman leader and later Britain's first female PM.

MARCH Daily Mirror's publication halts after 1,750 warehouse staff are dismissed, after unofficially walking out, causing the loss of half the paper's run of 3,200,000 copies.

APRIL In the budget, income tax rises for everyone, but a new scheme of family allowances for all children, brings some welcome relief.

MAY A coach crashes through Dibble's Bridge in Yorkshire, dropping 25ft into the river, killing 32 people and seriously injuring 14 others

JUNE In his absence after he disappeared, Lord Lucan is convicted of murdering his children's nanny at his wife's London home. (He was declared dead in 1999)

JULY The first phase of the extension of London Underground's Piccadilly line to Heathrow Airport is completed with the opening of Hatton Cross tube station.

AUGUST The 'Birmingham Six', were sentenced to life for the 1974 Birmingham pub bombings. (Their convictions were quashed by the Court of Appeal in 1991).

SEPTEMBER The London Hilton hotel is bombed by the IRA, killing two people and injuring 63 others.

OCTOBER West Yorkshire Police launch a hunt for the killer of 28-year-old prostitute Wilma McCann in Leeds. Later she is found to be the Yorkshire Ripper's first murder victim.

NOVEMBER The Employment Protection Act establishes Acas to arbitrate industrial disputes, extends jurisdiction of employment tribunals, establishes a Maternity Pay Fund and legislates against unfair dismissal.

DECEMBER The Sex Discrimination Act 1975 and the Equal Pay Act 1970, come into force aiming to end unequal pay of men and women in the workplace.

Films and Arts

Filmed on location at Martha's Vineyard in Massachusetts, Steven Spielberg's **Jaws** was the first film to be shot on the ocean, encountering many problems over budget and schedule. The shark's presence is mostly suggested at by John Williams' minimalist theme music, resulting in a tense thriller.

In total contrast the British comedy **Monty Python and The Holy Grail** is a story which parodies the Arthurian Legend, written by and starring the Python troupe. It grossed more than any British film screened in the US in 1975, and is considered one of the greatest comedy films of all time.

The American family series **Little House on The Prairie** first aired on TV in February, and **Kwa Zulu** opened at the New London Theatre in July, telling the story of two young lovers and the challenges they face within their tribe. Meanwhile on the Home Front, **Dad's Army** was selling out at The Shaftesbury Theatre.

Financial cuts at the BBC meant that on weekday afternoons trade test transmission cards were shown, unless there was live sports or schools programmes to transmit. However, our evenings became more exciting with a new series, **The Sweeney** starring John Thaw and Dennis Waterman.

1975 THE YEAR

Married in 1975, you were one of 56.2 million people living in Britain. This year, there were almost 381,000 marriages, a declining number since a boom in the 1960s, due in part to people delaying the age at which they married. There was also a clear shift *away* from the March wedding and a shift *towards* a summer wedding as a previous "tax break" had been removed and there was now no financial bonus for getting married before 5th April.

In 1975, the basic rate of income tax was 35% of earnings. Strikes and industrial action continued to cause headaches for the government, and financial ruin for some companies who had to close.

The IRA continued their campaign of bombing, but the public resolutely went about their daily lives as normal and the government forged ahead with its programme of building new houses to accommodate an ever-increasing population. Councils too, caught up in the fever of new building, sometimes swept away parts of our architectural heritage to replace it with something less pleasing to the eye.

The NHS was starting to creak, though politicians were quick to deny there were any problems, and equally determined to phase out pay beds.

Chopper bikes were a status symbol for children; space hoppers were still 'cool' and there were video games and colour TV featuring Hong Kong Phooey, Fawlty Towers and Dr No was the first Bond film to be shown on British television; Queen releases Bohemian Rhapsody and The Wizard of Oz (1939 film) is shown on British television for the first time.

How Much Did It Cost?

The Average Pay	£3,380 (£65 pw)
The Average House	£10,000
Loaf of White Bread	15p
Pint of Milk	7p
Pint of Beer	28p
Gallon of Petrol	73p (15p a litre)
Newspapers	5p
To Post a letter in UK	7p
12mnths Road Tax	£40
TV Licence	B/W £8 Colour £18

On 3rd November the Forties Field was inaugurated by Her Majesty Queen Elizabeth at Aberdeen. It is the largest oilfield to be discovered so far in the British sector of the North Sea.

YOU WERE MARRIED

POPULAR CULTURE

Silent film legend Charlie Chaplin at age 85, becomes Sir Charles, after a ceremony at Buckingham Palace. The film star was knighted in the New Year's Honours List.

Rocky Horror Picture Show

The **Rocky Horror Picture Show** released its musical comedy horror film based on the musical stage production. The story centres on a young couple whose car breaks down near a castle, where they search for help and find strangers in elaborate costumes celebrating. **Led Zeppelin** return to the UK to play five sold-out shows at Earls Court in London.

Gerald Seymour's thriller **Harry's Game** is published and later adapted for television; Agatha Christie's final Hercule Poirot novel **Curtain**, is the last novel published by Christie before her death.

The first episode of the popular sitcom **Fawlty Towers** is broadcast on BBC Two and the musical **Happy as a Sandbag** makes its debut in London.

The National Railway Museum opened in York, with historic and contemporary exhibits, as well as a library and archive of railway related material.

Shirley Conran's guide **Superwoman** a guide to saving stress, time and money is published. The Sunday Express describes it as *'A wise and witty book...Jam-packed with all manner of household hints and endless useful advice...It would make a splendid wedding present.'*

York National Railway Museum

1975

SPORTING HEADLINES

JANUARY Australia's Evonne Goolagong, a native Aborigine from New South Wales beat Czech champion Martina Navratilova to take the Women's Singles title in the **Australian Tennis Open**.

MARCH 'The Yukon Fox' Emmitt Peters won the Rookie of the Year Award in the **Iditarod Dog Sled Race** in the Yukon. A native Alaskan, he won his first ever race with lead dogs Nugget and Digger.

MAY The **FA Cup Final** was a London team derby, between West Ham who beat Fulham 2-0. The match was played to a crowd of 100,00 spectators at Wembley Stadium.

JUNE The first ever **World Cricket Cup** final at Lords Cricket Ground saw the West Indies beat Australia by 17 runs.

JULY Eddie Merckx, the Belgian cyclist in the **Tour de France** was subjected to violence at the hands of the French supporters, angry that a Belgian was in the lead ahead of their native entrant. He was punched in the kidneys by a spectator and fell from his bike. Sustaining a broken cheekbone he had to retire from the race. France's Bernard Thevenet went on to win the yellow jersey.

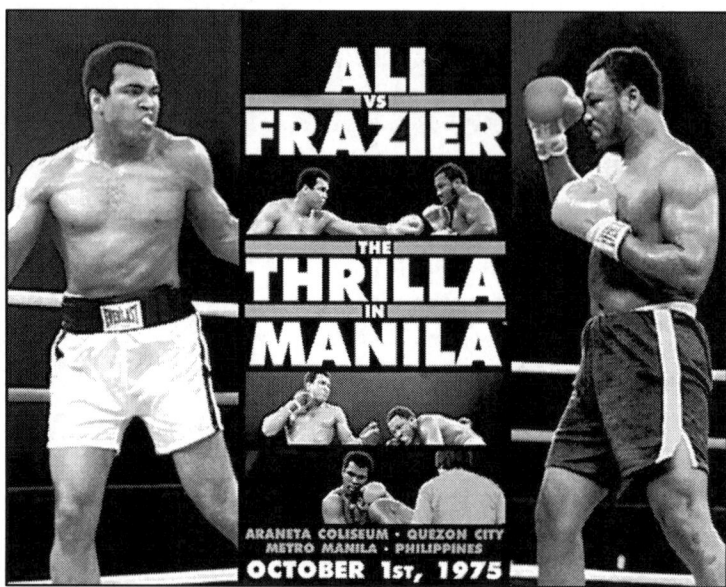

AUGUST In **Athletics**, New Zealander John Walker set a new world record becoming the first man to run a mile in 3mins 49.4secs

OCTOBER Muhammad Ali beat Joe Frazier to retain his **World Heavyweight Boxing** title in Manila, The Philippines. Known as 'The Thrilla in Manila' many regard this as the greatest fight in boxing history.

NOVEMBER Australia beat England 25-0 at Headingley, Leeds in the **Rugby League World Cup**.

SPORTING EVENTS

GRAHAM HILL F1 RACING CHAMPION

In November this year, Graham Hill and five other Embassy Hill executives, were killed when the Piper PA-23 Aztec aircraft he was piloting crashed in low-visibility conditions. Graham Hill was born in 1929 in Hampstead, and on leaving school, worked at Smith's Instruments as an apprentice engineer. He completed his National Service in the Royal Navy, rising to the rank of petty officer and after leaving the navy, he returned to work as a qualified engineer. He was a member of the London Rowing Club in the 50's, contesting twenty finals including the Grand Challenge Cup. Hill did not pass his driving test until he was 24 years old and described his first car as *'A wreck. A budding racing driver should own such a car, as it teaches delicacy, poise and anticipation, mostly the latter I think!'*

He made his racing debut in Formula Three aged 25, then joined Lotus in Formula One as a mechanic, before earning a driving debut with the team at the 1958 Monaco Grand Prix and securing a full-time contract. He was known for his race preparation, keeping records of the settings on his car and working long hours with his mechanics. In 1969 he became a five-time winner of the Monaco Grand Prix a record he held for 24 years. During the US Grand Prix he was seriously injured in a crash, breaking both of his legs. Typically, when asked soon after the crash if he wanted to pass on a message to his wife, Hill replied *'Just tell her that I won't be dancing for two weeks.'* A staunch campaigner for road safety, Hill presented a series for Thames Television entitled *Advanced Driving with Graham Hill* comprising six 30-minute programmes broadcast weekly in June and July 1974.

1975

THE FIRST REFERENDUM

Held on June 5, the first nationwide referendum in British history was held and focused on whether the United Kingdom should remain a member of the European Economic Community (EEC), commonly referred to as the Common Market. Britain had joined the EEC in 1973, but growing domestic scepticism about the economic and political implications of membership led to demands for a public vote.

Prime Minister Harold Wilson's Labour government, elected in 1974, promised to renegotiate the terms of Britain's membership and put it to a referendum. The campaign saw heated debates, with proponents emphasising economic benefits and access to European markets, while opponents highlighted concerns over national sovereignty and loss of control over domestic policies. The result was a decisive 67.2% vote in favour of remaining in the EEC, with a turnout of 64.5%.

FAWLTY TOWERS

This year saw the introduction to our television screens of Basil and Sybil Fawlty. Set in Fawlty Towers, a fictional hotel in Torquay, in Devon, the plot centres on the dysfunctional nature of the owner, Basil, his bossy wife Sybil, a hapless Spanish waiter Manuel who speaks very little English and the long suffering, sensible, chamber maid Polly, doing their best to run the hotel with farcical situations, eccentric guests and very odd tradespeople.

The show was inspired by the Gleneagles Hotel in Torquay, where the Monty Python cast had previously stayed. The owner, Donald Sinclair, on whom John Cleese based his character Basil, was known for his snobbish and eccentric attitude towards guests, treating them as though they were a hindrance to his running of the hotel – he allegedly threw Eric Idle's briefcase out of a window!

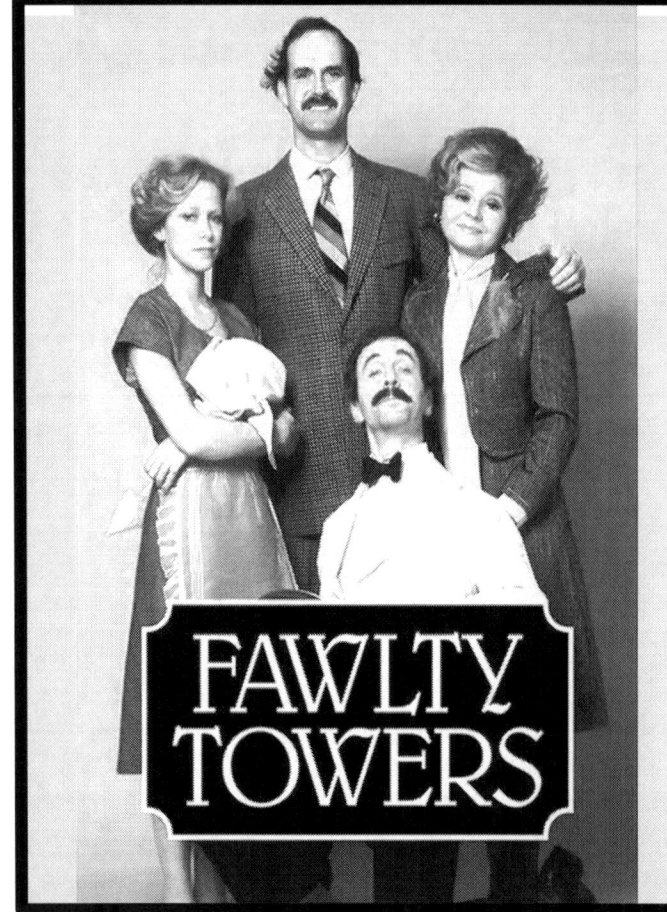

CULTURAL EVENTS

BOHEMIAN RHAPSODY

Although reactions were initially mixed, Bohemian Rhapsody has been acclaimed one of the greatest songs of all time, and it is often regarded as Queen's signature song. Released this year, it began life sometime in the late 60s when Freddie Mercury was studying at Ealing Art College and scribbled ideas for songs on scraps of paper.

At one time called 'The Cowboy Song' – maybe because of the line, 'Mama … just killed a man' – he banged it out on the piano, full of gaps where he explained that 'something operatic would happen here'. He later said, *"Bohemian Rhapsody was basically three songs that I wanted to put out, and I just put the three together."* It was recorded between August and September and parodies elements of opera with grandiose choruses, and Italian operatic style phrases.

BARBIE

The 1970's marked a significant shift in the world of Barbie, and it was a time when her fashion and design took a bold turn, mirroring the dynamic changes in women's roles and styles in society. The decade introduced some of the most memorable Barbie dolls, each embodying the spirit of the era, and saw Barbie taking on various careers, from being an athlete to a surgeon.

Barbie broke stereotypes and encouraged young girls to dream big and aspire for new roles in society. This was the seventeenth year of production for Barbie and Mattel decided to capitalise on the upcoming 1976 Winter Olympics in Austria, by releasing their Gold Medal series of four dolls – Gold Medal Barbie and Ken Skiers, Gold Medal Barbie Skater, and Winter Sports.

1975

THE HOMEBREW COMPUTER CLUB

The Homebrew Computer Club was a highly influential gathering of technology enthusiasts, engineers, and hobbyists, and played a pivotal role in fostering the development of the personal computer industry. Its members shared a passion for exploring the potential of microcomputers, which were just beginning to emerge as accessible technologies.

It was started by Gordon French and Fred Moore who met at the Community Computer Center in Menlo Park, a city in Silicon Valley and the club became a vibrant forum for exchanging ideas, sharing technical knowledge, and showcasing innovations. Members would often present their projects and discuss emerging technologies, creating a collaborative atmosphere that spurred innovation.

Among its notable members were Steve Wozniak and Steve Jobs, who developed the Apple I computer, which they debuted at the club. This collaboration eventually led to the founding of Apple Inc., marking a turning point in the personal computing revolution.

The Apple 1 Computer

THE APOLLO-SOYUZ PROJECT

In July, the first crewed international space mission carried out jointly by the United States and the Soviet Union symbolised a historic collaboration between the United States and the Soviet Union, paving the way for future international cooperation in space. Millions of people around the world watched on television as an American Apollo spacecraft, docked with a Soviet Soyuz capsule.

The project, and its handshake in space, was a symbol of détente between the two superpowers amid the Cold War. The American astronauts, Stafford, Brand, and Slayton, and the Soviet cosmonauts, Leonov and Kubasov, performed both joint and separate scientific experiments, including using the Apollo module to block out the sun to allow instruments on the Soyuz to take photographs of the solar corona.

Science And Nature

The Chacoan Peccary

By 1930 the Chacoan peccary, also known as the 'skunk pig', was thought to be extinct and the only traces found were fossils. However local sightings four years ago in a remote area of Paraguay, have been confirmed this year by Western scientists.

Small herds are confined to hot, dry areas of the Gran Chaco where only succulents and thorny bushes thrive. The peccary has well developed sinuses to combat dry, dusty conditions and small feet, which allows manoeuvrability among spiny plants.

They are vulnerable to human activity, and herd numbers are already decreasing due to habitat loss where their territory is being quickly transformed into large Texas-style ranches. For this reason, a population is now being established in North American and European zoos.

Standpipes In The Streets

The drought of 1975 in Britain was one of the most significant weather events of the decade, marked by an extended period of unusually dry and warm conditions. It followed an already dry 1974, with rainfall in many areas of the UK significantly below average.

The impact of the drought was widespread. Rivers, reservoirs, and groundwater levels fell dramatically, leading to water shortages in many regions and in some areas, restrictions were imposed, including hosepipe bans and water rationing.

The agricultural sector was particularly hard-hit with crops failing and livestock suffering from a lack of pasture and water, which in turn drove up prices in the shops. The government established a drought action committee encouraging water conservation with their slogan "Save It".

1975 LIFESTYLES OF

Increasing Prosperity

In 1975 unemployment was rising rapidly and job security was no longer guaranteed as businesses suffered under a recession. However apart from the lowest income bracket, an increasing number of the population had credit cards, paying off part of their credit balance each month. This meant that even with uncertainty and static income, people could continue to buy consumables as well as daily necessities on credit. Television was now the major source of entertainment in the home, and advertising exerted increasing pressure on us to have the perfect lifestyle and home, stylish clothes, and better cars.

Women's weekly magazines were sold at every newsagent and filled with recipes, fashion ideas, diet plans, and housekeeping tips they were considered one of a housewife's 'little treats' when she went shopping. Many towns still had a weekly market with a mixture of fresh food stalls, and plants and there were fabric and haberdashery stalls selling everything for home dressmaking, using patterns by Butterick or Simplicity, or with the help of one of the many sewing books by Ann Ladbury.

Changing Tastes

Laura Ashley inspired us to embrace Victoriana, with flowery prints and muted colours and Golden Hands magazines and books gave easy instructions on crafts like macrame or crochet to embellish our homes or make our clothes more stylish. Most towns had a department store, and a couple of supermarkets such as Fine Fare, Asda or Sainsbury's whilst in the Midlands and Southern counties you might also have a Bejam store for frozen foods.

Everyday People

New Food Ideas

By 1975, more people were being exposed to new food ideas, either through travel abroad or through the cookery programmes which were becoming very popular on television. One cooking show that aired in the UK was 'Take Kerr', a daily five-minute series hosted by ' The Galloping Gourmet', Graham Kerr. The show featured a different recipe each day and was characterised by its lighter-calorie recipes and Christian elements. The theme song was the hymn 'This Is the Day the Lord Has Made'. Other cooking programmes featured chef Phillip Harben, or the iconic duo, Fanny and Johnny Craddock. Fanny with her flame red hair and startling make up both encouraged us to try new things and appalled us with some of her strange concoctions, while poor henpecked Johnny just elicited our sympathy.

Favourite Foods

In the supermarket, Instant noodles and Vesta curries filled the shelves whilst party food included cocktail onions, pineapple pieces and cheese cubes on cocktail sticks, and prawn cocktails with salad cream and tomato ketchup. Black forest gateaux, Arctic Roll, Angel Delight, and sherry trifle were popular desserts. Meanwhile the English Tourist Board was encouraging restaurants to include more British dishes on their menus in the face of our growing love of foreign, spicy, food. One of the final bastions of the English Working Man's menu had to be 'The Greasy Spoon' found at every transport-caff, dockyard, industrial area or area of habitation that was not in the process of being 'refined'. Bangers and fried bread, double egg and chips, doorstep butties and beans were the standard all-day menu, washed down with half a pint of freshly brewed Tetley's Tea.

January 1st – 7th 1975

IN THE NEWS

Wednesday 1 — **"Smaller Bags of Sugar"** Pensioners and poorer families may struggle to pay the price rise of 28p for a 2lb bag of sugar. The Government will speed up metrication, making smaller half-kilo bags available.

Thursday 2 — **"New Lifeboat"** The 21st International Boat Show featured the new self-righting lifeboat, to mark the 150th anniversary of the foundation of the Royal National Life-boat Institution.

Friday 3 — **"Highway Code Out of Date"** The AA say the Highway Code is out of date and the public has poor knowledge of its contents. Since publication in 1969 there have been 17 changes to road markings, street signs and guidance to road users.

Saturday 4 — **"Stamps and Phone Bills To Rise"** Telephone charges are going up, with the average phone bill increasing to over £64 a year. 1st class post will increase to 7p and second-class to 5p.

Sunday 5 — **"Poet's Home to Stay in Welsh Hands"** Dylan Thomas's home has been bought by the Wales Tourist Board and an educational trust and will become a museum. Most of the £23,500 sale price was donated by the Tourist Board.

Monday 6 — **"Nerve Gas Fear"** MPs are questioning why the formula for a lethal nerve gas has been taken off the secret list. It has been suggested that the substance could easily be manufactured by a student in a university laboratory.

Tuesday 7 — **"Wasting Energy"** Britain wastes more energy at home and in industry than other European countries. Scientists estimate that demand could be cut by a tenth in three years without lowering the standard of living.

HERE IN BRITAIN

"P.G. Wodehouse KBE"

P. G. Wodehouse, author of the Jeeves comedy novels, who is 93 and holds dual British-American citizenship, is to be made KBE - Knight Commander of the Most Excellent Order of the British Empire.
The knighthood will be seen by many as an official indication that he no longer remains in the shadows due to the criticisms aimed at him during WWII, when the Nazis made propaganda out of his broadcasts from Berlin. Mr Wodehouse, who is too frail to travel to England, will go to the British Embassy in Washington to receive the award.

AROUND THE WORLD

"Tasman Bridge Disaster"

A large container ship collided with several pylons of the Tasman Bridge in Hobart, Tasmania, causing a large section of the bridge to collapse onto the ship and into the river below. As the collision occurred on the evening of 5th of January, which was a Sunday evening, there was less traffic on the bridge, but twelve people were killed. Two drivers managed to stop at the edge, but not before their front wheels had dropped over the broken bridge deck. Fortunately, both drivers managed to ease themselves out of their cars to safety.

Hogmanay

While New Year is celebrated throughout Britain, the North of the country takes partying to a whole new level, particularly in Scotland, where Christmas takes second place to the more important 'Hogmanay'. While most Brits are back to work on the 2nd January, Scotland gets an additional Bank Holiday on that day either to continue the festivities, or to recover from them.

The tradition of 'first-footing' in Scotland and Northern England refers to the first person to cross the threshold after midnight on New Years Day. Strict New Year etiquette states that the 'first-footer' must either be a brand-new visitor to the house after midnight, or have left the building by the back door before the first stroke of midnight, re-entering via the front door after the chimes have finished. A first footer must be male, and cannot arrive at a house empty-handed, for he is seen as a bringer of good fortune for the coming year. Armed with symbolic gifts of coal, shortbread and money; gifts which ensure the household's warmth, food supply, wealth, and good cheer for the coming year, and he must be given food and drink in return by the inhabitants of the house. The first footer must also be dark haired – a superstition which may go back to the time of Vikings when the arrival of a blond stranger at your door would be the cause of fear and alarm.

As with many winter festivals, fire plays a prominent part; these days with fireworks, but traditional New Year ceremonies involved people running through the streets carrying lighted torches. These were made of animal hides wrapped around sticks and ignited to produce smoke to ward off evil spirits – the smoking stick is known as a 'Hogmanay.'

January 8th – 14th 1975

IN THE NEWS

Wednesday 8 — **"Heathrow Hijack"** A hijacker with a fake gun held a plane's crew hostage for 8 hours, but was later arrested by police while trying to escape with the £100,000 ransom money.

Thursday 9 — **"No Longer Beatles"** The Beatles & Co partnership was finally dissolved at a High Court hearing, eight years after it was first formed and five years after the group split up.

Friday 10 — **"Cutting Pollution"** A filter that will reduce lead pollution has been developed by the Transport and Road Research Laboratory together with four private companies. Fitted to new cars, it can halve lead emissions in five years. In nine years, with the demise of older cars, emissions would be negligible.

Saturday 11 — **"New Oil Platforms"** The Government has sanctioned three more Scottish sites for concrete oil-production platforms, at Hunterston, on the shores of Loch Fyne, and a third near Campbeltown.

Sunday 12 — **"Knotty Ash Recognised"** Marking European Architectural Heritage Year, a gazetteer of Merseyside's industrial heritage is being compiled, to include Knotty Ash Brewery, Hartley's castellated jam factory, Aintree's clock tower, and Birkenhead public baths.

Monday 13 — **"Heating Controls"** New Government regulations setting a maximum temperature of 20°C (68°F) in shops and offices and the use of daytime electricity for advertising signs took effect today.

Tuesday 14 — **"Arabian Flats"** Consort Lodge, a fully air-conditioned block of flats with three-bedroom suites, large reception rooms, and balconies overlooking Regent's Park, has been sold to an Arabian government. The estate agents expected to sell the flats individually and were surprised to receive an offer for the whole block.

HERE IN BRITAIN

"Disappointed Skiers"

Even in Speyside, which is normally bleak, the whole country is basking in the mildest January for fifty years. The slopes of Cairngorm, which by now should be covered in snow and skiers, remain black with earth and rocks. One ski school has sent its instructors home and told them to return when the snow comes.

By mid-January, between four and five thousand skiers would expect to be using the ski lift facilities on Cairngorm, but this year beginners are queuing up for lessons on an artificial slope in the Aviemore centre.

AROUND THE WORLD

"End of a Tradition"

King Carl Gustaf XVI was merely a figurehead when he opened the Swedish parliament under a new constitution this week. For the past 400 years the occasion has been marked with ceremony and royal spectacle, but the king, dressed in a plain dark suit, simply rode up an escalator to the modernistic parliamentary chamber to be invited by the Speaker to declare this year's session open. He then sat to listen to the opening address, previously read by the reigning monarch as Head of State, read by the Prime Minister.

Liberty's Of London

Visitors to London are enjoying this year's mild January weather and thousands are visiting the famous Liberty store on Regent Street, both to view the building itself and to shop for the iconic Liberty print goods. The store was founded in 1875 by Arthur Lasenby Liberty, who borrowed £2,000 from his future father-in-law and bought the building. At first an importer of fabrics and objets d'arts, Arthur later collaborated with William Morris and began selling his own distinctive brand of fabrics in 1880.

The shop was completely redesigned in 1924 when a building firm was given a sum of £198,000 to create today's 'Mock Tudor' emporium. It was constructed from the timbers of two ancient ships, HMS Impregnable, built from 3,040 100-year-old oaks from the New Forest, and HMS Hindustan. More than 24,000 cubic feet of ships' timbers were used, including the decks, which became the shop flooring. Designed to feel like a home, each atrium was surrounded by smaller rooms, complete with fireplaces and furnishings made at the Liberty furniture workshops in Archway, London. Outside there is a gilded 4ft high, copper, weathervane of The Mayflower, which took pilgrims to the New World in 1620. The Liberty Clock on Kingly Street depicts St. George & The Dragon and tells us "*No minute gone comes ever back again, take heed and see ye nothing do in vain*" while inside on the old staircase, carved memorials remember the Liberty staff who died in World War II. There are Shields of Shakespeare and portraits of Henry VIII's six wives dotted about and carved wooden animals are hidden throughout the store. Sadly, Arthur Liberty never saw his dream realised, dying seven years before it opened but his statue stands at the Flower Shop entrance.

January 15th – 21st 1975

IN THE NEWS

Wednesday 15 — **"Taxes Instead of Rates"** The National Union of Ratepayers' Associations want rates replaced with a local income tax. This would make 9m more people liable to pay, *'thus reducing the sum required from each of the existing 16m ratepayers by more than 40%'*.

Thursday 16 — **"Search for Water"** The Anglian Water Authority have begun work on drilling 34 boreholes, costing £1 million, near Bury St Edmunds in a search for new water reserves for East Anglia.

Friday 17 — **"Ceasefire Ends"** English cities are expected to bear the brunt of the Provisional IRA's renewed bombing campaign following the breakdown of the 25-day old ceasefire.

Saturday 18 — **"Speed Traps Detected"** A company that makes miniature radio receivers, which give advanced warnings of X-band transmissions, was prosecuted at St. Albans. 150,000 devices have already been sold to the public to *'help motorists detect radar traps.'*

Sunday 19 — **"Dangerous Games"** A primary school playing field in Langney near Eastbourne, which was laid out on the site of an old refuse tip, has been closed by the council after toxic waste was discovered in water running through the field.

Monday 20 — **"Machine Gun Attacks"** Machine gun attacks were made on two London hotel restaurants, injuring eight people. Both restaurants are popular with the Jewish community and police are treating them as anti-Semitic attacks.

Tuesday 21 — **"Climbers Rescued"** Two climbers were rescued after being trapped on a ledge on a cliff face on Ben Nevis for 24 hours, in 100 mph winds and driving snow. They were lowered 300ft to safety by the Lochaber Mountain Rescue Team, helped by police and RAF volunteers.

HERE IN BRITAIN

"Family Savings"

Fine Fare supermarket in York did not make a profit for seven months because of the activities of a family gang. 'The spider in the centre of the web', was a mother of five who worked on a cash till in the store and gave members of her family 'unofficial discounts' by undercharging them for groceries. Nine members of the family appeared before magistrates charged with theft and falsifying till rolls. It is understood that several thousand pounds was involved; one relative paid only £5 for £15 worth of goods three times a week.

AROUND THE WORLD

Around The World "Space Mountain"

A new ride has opened at Disney World in Florida. It is a space themed indoor roller coaster, the first to be operated by computer. The ride takes place in darkness, with special lighting and sound effects, while full size astronaut figures, suspended upside-down, give the illusion of zero-gravity. Projected images of planets and the milky way are seen from the trains as they climb the lift-hill before plunging through twists and turns around the mountain in darkness, finally ending with the trains passing through a red and orange swirling wormhole to the unloading station.

Girls In Rugby

Founded in 1567 as a free grammar school for local boys by Lawrence Sheriff, who had made his fortune supplying groceries to Queen Elizabeth I, Rugby is one of the oldest independent schools in Britain and the birthplace of rugby football. This month marked a major change in a 400-year-old tradition, when girls were admitted as 6th form pupils for the first time.

The school's most famous headmaster was Thomas Arnold, in post from 1828 to 1841, whose emphasis on moral and religious principle, was widely admired and seen as the blueprint for Victorian public schools. When French educator Pierre de Coubertin, visited the school, he cited it as one of the main inspirations for his notable achievement - the founding of the modern Olympic Games in 1896 and the school has been immortalised in Thomas Hughes 1857 novel *'Tom Brown's School Days'*. It was a Rugby schoolboy in 1823 who first picked up a football and ran with it, inventing the new sport and, in 1845, a committee of the boys wrote the *'Laws of Football as Played At Rugby School'* which was the first published set of laws for any code of football. The legend of the origin of the game is commemorated by a plaque.

Three girls were in the first admission this year. The current headmaster, Jim Woodhouse, was under pressure from parents whose sons were at Rugby and wanted their daughters to attend, too. He wrote a paper for his Board of Governors, which was approved, and on Speech Day announced that the sisters of day boys (only the day boys) and the daughters of masters would be allowed to attend the school – as day girls. They wore trousers and blazers at first, but later swapped the trousers for maxi skirts, teamed with jackets.

January 22ND - 28TH 1975

IN THE NEWS

Wednesday 22 — **"No Criticism Please"** The BBC has received many telephone complaints after the broadcast of a film report, in which the Labour MP for Fife Central was critical about a suspected understated total of the monarchy's financial assets.

Thursday 23 — **"Building Slump"** According to the Government, the building industry should expect a worsening of the present slump, which will continue well into 1976.

Friday 24 — **"Train Crash"** It is thought that the theft of car engines and parts from freight cars found to have their doors open, caused a London to Glasgow express to crash with a train travelling from Manchester, just south of Watford Junction. One man was killed and 32 people injured.

Saturday 25 — **"Dum-Dum Bullets"** The Home Secretary has asked for a ban on the use of dum-dum bullets in the .38 revolvers used by the police. The bullet has already been banned by the Hague convention, owing to the violence of its impact on the human body.

Sunday 26 — **"New Archbishop of Canterbury"** During his enthronement in Canterbury cathedral, the new Archbishop, Dr Coggan, took the oath on the priceless Gospels of St. Augustine which date from the 6th Century.

Monday 27 — **"IRA Bombs"** A total of 26 people were hurt in bombings in London and Manchester. The London blasts were at Gieves, in Old Bond Street; a disused gasworks at Enfield; a chemical plant at Ponders End; a jeweller's shop in Kensington High Street; and the Army and Navy store in Victoria Street.

Tuesday 28 — **"Doctors to Strike"** The Medical Practitioners' Union, which represent almost 5,000 doctors, called for a 24-hour stoppage in a bid for improved pay.

HERE IN BRITAIN

"Amin Calling the Shots"

President Idi Amin of Uganda announced that he will visit Britain in August and asked the Queen to arrange for him to meet the leaders of the *'liberation movements'* of Scotland, Wales and Northern Ireland, for him to give them advice.

He also wants to meet the British Asians whom *'I booted out of my country in September 1972.'* Amin referred to Britain's ailing economy and told the Queen, that with this advance warning of his visit, *"I hope there will be at least during my stay, a steady and reliable supply of essential commodities'*

AROUND THE WORLD

"Wombles"

A newly discovered animal, found in South Australia still has no official Latin name. It is a small mouse-like creature which suckles its young in a pouch, like all marsupials. The young are about half the size of a little fingernail and adults grow to 10 cm from nose to tail and, at first sight, could be taken for the common British shrew.

Instead of the typical large, chisel-like front teeth and blunt nose of rodents, this animal has a distinctive arrangement of small, sharp teeth and a long, pointed nose, rather like the fictional Wombles.

BURNS NIGHT

Piping in the haggis.
The INSET shows a portrait of Robbie Burns.

Robert Burns was born in Ayrshire on the west coast of Scotland in 1759, the eldest of seven children. His birthday on 25th January, has been marked for over 200 years with feasting and recitations of his works among Scots and Hibernophiles all over the world. His father was a poor and relatively unsuccessful tenant farmer, and Robert's childhood was marked by poverty and hard manual work. Educated to read and write mainly by his self-taught father, he wrote many poems and songs in Scottish dialect while working as a farm labourer. It was only later on in life that his work about the themes of love and nature, was published and became very popular. Burns fathered twelve children to four different women, the last being born on the day he died, 21st July 1796.

Burns Night Suppers are held the world over, and in Scotland are more widely observed than that of its patron saint, St. Andrew, on 30th November. The suppers generally follow the same format with a welcome to the guests, and announcements, following which the 'Selkirk Grace' is recited. Then the haggis, the 'great chieftain o' the pudding-race' a traditional meat and herb pudding, is brought in on a silver tray, piped in by a bagpipe player. 'Address To a Haggis' is recited while the haggis is served with neeps and tatties, as potatoes and turnips are called, and drams of whisky. Afterwards many of his other poems will be recited and often there will be dancing. The evening finishes with the singing of the traditional song 'Auld Lang Syne' which Burns based on an older Scottish folk song. To this day it is traditionally sung to bid farewell to the old year at the stroke of midnight on Hogmanay (New Year's Eve).

JAN 29TH - FEB 4TH 1975

IN THE NEWS

Wednesday 29 — **"Busmen's Strike?"** Following a spate of assaults on bus crews, and the death of a conductor 10 days ago, the TGW Union, has called for a one-day strike by its 160,000 members to demand that action is taken to prevent further attacks.

Thursday 30 — **"Licence Fees Up"** TV licences are to be increased. Black and white will increase by only £1, from £7 to £8 to minimise the effect on pensioners and low-income households, but colour licences will rise from £12 to £18.

Friday 31 — **"Iconic Plant Sold"** The Meriden factory have sold the Norton Villiers Triumph's motorcycle plant to The Meriden Workers' Cooperative for £4.2m. The cooperative was formed in 1973 to save the factory from closure.

Saturday Feb 1 — **"Objectors Causing Havoc"** The public enquiry into a new road through Epping Forest has been halted by environmental objectors. They say there will be no increase in future traffic. The delays could lengthen the enquiry and increase costs by £500,000.

Sunday 2 — **"Aid for Historic Churches"** The Government has agreed in principle to donate £1m a year for the upkeep of historic churches that are still in ecclesiastical use, regardless of denomination. Cathedrals will not receive the subsidy.

Monday 3 — **"Irish Government Calls Their Bluff"** Despite the possibility that two IRA hunger strikers at Portlaoise Jail may starve themselves to death soon the Government has decided they won't give in to their demand for political prisoner status.

Tuesday 4 — **"Levy for Liability"** Action on Smoking and Health (ASH) say that cigarette manufacturers should pay compensation for the health damage caused by smoking. This to be funded by a 3p – 5p levy on each pack of cigarettes.

HERE IN BRITAIN

"M62 Bombing Memorial"

Wreaths were placed at a memorial to the 12 victims of the M62 coach bombing, erected at the Hartshead Moor service station two miles from where the bomb exploded.
Twelve months ago, 12 people, including a couple and their two children, were killed when a bomb exploded in a coach carrying servicemen and their families from Manchester to Catterick camp, Yorkshire. The organiser of the memorial spoke of bomb threats to himself and his family after the appeal started last October, *'telephone calls from people speaking with Irish accents.'*

AROUND THE WORLD

"Haicheng Earthquake"

Because early warning signs and small tremors were heeded, much of Haicheng in NE China was evacuated before the main earthquake struck and therefore, few died in collapsed buildings, despite the destruction being extensive.
However, over 300 people froze to death, and thousands suffered frostbite, as evacuees were living in makeshift tents, sleeping on bed sheets and straw on the frozen ground. Then a huge fire broke out amongst the evacuees' shelters, killing a further 350 people.

CHINESE NEW YEAR

兔 1975
Wood Rabbit

THE YEAR OF THE RABBIT

The Chinese New Year of the Rabbit began life with a big bang. Gerrard Street, Soho, the Chinatown of London, was thronged for their festival to celebrate the end of the Year of the Tiger and the beginning of the Year of the Rabbit. Barrages of firecrackers imported from Hong Kong were let off in the car park at the end of the street, filling the afternoon with acrid gunpowder smoke and the shrieks of children. Every shop was festooned with red lanterns, scarlet banners and Chinese poems.

Fishing lines baited with strings of lettuce were dangled from upper windows for the lion of the traditional Chinese lion dance, a terrifying but herbivorous beast of many colours, who came dancing down the street, leaping and shaking his head in time to cymbals and drums. A lion-tamer in a round red mask guided him from lettuce to lettuce with a straw fan in each hand. In Chinese culture, the rabbit has the unique characteristic of waiting for an opportune moment and leaping into action. The Loon Fung supermarket had pictures of the Rabbit on show beside Peking red wine and boxes of shrimp chips. Every child entering the street was given a handful of sweets and a gas-filled balloon.

One of the distributors of sweets said that the essential point of Chinese New Year was that it should be a family reunion. *"There is no special food that we eat at new year, just an enormous lot of food."* When Gerrard Street began its history in the seventeenth century it was a military parade ground. The first Chinese restaurant was opened in 1926 and now almost every shop has become Chinese. From all the shops Chinese music tinkled, gongs sounded and the scents of fried prawn balls and honey barbecued pork ribs spiced the air and happy crowds surged along.

February 5th – 11th 1975

IN THE NEWS

Wednesday 5 — **"Listening In"** Workmen dismantling part of a room at the Communist Party HQ in London, discovered a 10-year-old bugging device in panelling, capable of transmitting conversations to listeners 50 yards away.

Thursday 6 — **"Fitting Ceremony"** The Queen's uncle, the Duke of Norfolk, was buried in the family's Fitzalan Chapel of Arundel Castle, the repository of the bodies of his ancestors, earl marshals and great potentates of the realm stretching back to the early Middle Ages. As Master of Royal Ceremonies, the Duke had planned many of the funeral details himself.

Friday 7 — **"Toe the Comprehensive Line"** Councils who refuse to draw up schemes for comprehensive education will be forced to do so, by legislation if necessary. The Minister said, *'we will not tolerate deliberate defiance and any scheme designed to perpetuate selection, however disguised, is completely unacceptable'*.

Saturday 8 — **"Stowaways Want Asylum"** Romanian Officials have complained because they were denied access to three stowaways, currently in Pentonville Prison Hospital being treated for dehydration. Dockers found them stowed away on a cargo vessel.

Sunday 9 — **"Laker's Skytrain"** The Civil Aviation Authority has decided not to revoke the licence for the Skytrain service between London and New York. Passengers can book at short notice for a one way fare of £55, excluding meals.

Monday 10 — **"Indefinite Ceasefire"** The IRA has declared an indefinite ceasefire in Northern Ireland and Great Britain. In a statement from Dublin, the organisation appears to be working towards a permanent cessation of violence.

Tuesday 11 — **"Fact or Fiction"** About 2,000 people gathered outside Birmingham Cathedral to watch the filming of the fictitious wedding of 'Meg Richardson' played by Noele Gordon and 'Hugh Mortimer' played by John Bentley, in ATV's popular 'soap opera' Crossroads.

HERE IN BRITAIN

"Pop Exhaustion"

The Scottish pop group from Edinburgh, the Bay City Rollers, have cancelled their European tour next month because two members have collapsed from nervous exhaustion.

They are now one of the biggest selling acts in Britain, with their distinctive style of dress, featuring calf-length tartan trousers and tartan scarves. 'Rollermania' is on the rise all over Britain, but fans are having difficulty keeping up with 'all things tartan' as most shops have run out of tartan fabric!

AROUND THE WORLD

"I Do – Times 1,800"

The largest wedding ever, took place in Seoul, South Korea, when 1800 couples from over 21 countries were married simultaneously by Rev. Sun Myung Moon, founder of the Unification Church which teaches that God transcends all national and racial barriers, and that the Kingdom of Heaven can be built on earth through God-centred family units.

Couples in the 'Moonies' as the church is known, are matched by church authorities and may only meet a few days before the ceremony.

Shrove Tuesday

This week held Shrove Tuesday, the day before Ash Wednesday, when people traditionally went to confession to be 'shriven' or absolved of their sins before the Lenten fast. A bell would be rung to call people to confession, which became known as the 'Pancake Bell' and is still rung today. Any foods which weren't allowed during the fast had to be eaten up by midnight on the Tuesday or thrown out. The eggs were made into pancakes on the Tuesday and from this developed the custom of holding Pancake Races.

It has been suggested that the origins of the tradition came from a housewife in Olney, Buckinghamshire in 1445. The woman had been so busy making pancakes that she lost track of time, which led to her running to church still carrying her frying pan when she heard the bells ringing to signal the 11am service. Olney is one of the many towns that still have the traditional Pancake Race held each Shrove Tuesday, and which was won this year by a schoolgirl, Sally Ann Faulkner.

But racing with a hot frying pan is only one of the traditional activities on this day. 'Old rules' football games, where the goals can be several miles, or villages apart, are still held in Alnwick and Sedgefield in the Northeast, Atherstone in Warwickshire, and Ashbourne in Derbyshire. The game is played with an indeterminate number of players, over an unspecified area, and there are no rules, whatsoever. It is certainly not a game for the faint hearted, and injuries are quite common. In Scarborough the day is known as 'Skipping Day' and everyone assembles on the promenade to skip. Long ropes are stretched across the road and there might be ten or more people skipping on one rope, girls and grown women together.

February 12th - 18th 1975

IN THE NEWS

Wednesday 12   "**Mrs Thatcher Wins Outright**" Margaret Thatcher has become the first woman to lead a British political party and to become a potential Prime Minister. She won an outright victory for the leadership over four male challengers.

Thursday 13   "**Changing Habits**" The Health Minister, Dr. David Owen, stated that following the increase in tax on tobacco in March 1974, the sales of cigarettes started to decrease, and the trend seems to be continuing.

Friday 14   "**Bumper Mailbag**" Many Valentine cards arrived at the Commons office of Mrs Margaret Thatcher, the new Tory leader. One from an astrologer, predicted that she would become Prime Minister.

Saturday 15   "**Missing Boy Found**" A 15-year-old boy who spent four days in a plastic survival bag on the Yorkshire Moors, has emerged safe and well. He survived on three packet soups, three eggs and a carton of orange drink.

Sunday 16   "**Royal Visit**" The Queen and the Duke of Edinburgh have arrived in Bermuda on the first leg of their Caribbean tour. Despite a general strike in Hamilton, the island's capital, they were given a royal welcome.

Monday 17   "**Hunger Strike Ends**" The hunger strike by IRA prisoners at Curragh Military Hospital has ended. The most seriously ill prisoners came close to death but are now being administered glucose and water to aid their recovery.

Tuesday 18   "**Golden Eagles Back**" Ornithologists are guarding a pair of golden eagles which have returned to an eyrie in the Lake District. They are said to be England's only nesting pair of the birds of prey.

HERE IN BRITAIN

"New Weather Centre"

A new European Centre for Medium Range Weather Forecasts is to be sited at Shinfield Park, near Reading and will be one of the world's largest weather prediction and climate change monitoring organisations.

The running costs will be mainly met by the EU, The centre's purpose is to improve medium-range forecasting, as well as research into broadcasting techniques and providing advanced meteorological training for the staff of the member states, with considerable benefits for weather dependent industries such as agriculture, construction and shipping.

AROUND THE WORLD

"Vatican Stops Birth Control Book"

The Vatican has ordered all copies of a book on family planning written by a Roman Catholic international organisation to be destroyed. The organisation is now facing the possibility of legal proceedings from the contributors if it is withheld from the public.

The Vatican's complaints are not specific, but it is believed that exception has been taken to a section on the 'morality of contraception'. The book does not attack the Pope's teaching on birth control, but asks questions, and puts forward different views inviting different opinions.

Women in Westminster

Margaret Thatcher (top left), Nancy Astor (top right), Constance Markievicz (bottom right) and Florence Paton (bottom left).

On February 11th, 1975, Margaret Thatcher became the first woman to lead a political party in Britain after defeating both the current leader Edward Heath, and his preferred successor William Whitelaw.

Women have walked the corridors of Westminster in the pursuit of reform and women's' rights for many years. Some are remembered for their daring, others for breaking new ground. Suffragettes were asked to boycott the 1911 census because 'if they didn't count enough to have a vote, then 'neither shall they be counted'. Emily Wilding Davison chose to hide in a Westminster broom cupboard on that night to avoid appearing on any census form and was discovered by cleaners next morning.

Women aged 30 were given the vote in 1918 after World War I, in time for the General Election. The first woman to be elected to the House of Commons was Constance Markievicz, an Irish nationalist and revolutionary. A founding member of the Irish Citizen Army she took part in the Easter Rising of 1916, but as she was in Holloway Prison at the time of her election, she never took her seat. The first woman to actually take her seat in parliament, in 1919, was Nancy, Viscountess Astor, whose 2nd marriage gave her a title and a taste for politics. She represented Plymouth Sutton until 1945. Florence Paton she became the first woman to chair a debate on the Floor of the House of Commons in 1948. Margaret Bondfield was made the first female cabinet minister, and privy counsellor in 1929, and just after WWII became the first woman to preside over the whole House of Commons as Chairman of Committees, although she didn't occupy the Speaker's Chair. This privilege was not given to a woman until 1970 when Margaret Anderson became Deputy Speaker.

FEBRUARY 19TH - 25TH 1975

IN THE NEWS

Wednesday 19 — **"Ferry Blockade"** The Dover car ferry was turned back when 70 inshore fishing vessels began blocking the entrance to Boulogne harbour, as French fisherman staged a 72-hour strike over low fish prices.

Thursday 20 — **"Hospital Strike"** An appeal has been made to striking Welsh hospital staff to return to normal work, shortly before the discharge of a patient whose admission as a private patient to the Swansea hospital, had caused the dispute.

Friday 21 — **"Solar Power"** In a scheme launched by Pilkington Brothers, nine fuel efficient houses for the elderly, that will use only solar energy for heating, are to be built on Merseyside at a cost of £140,000 each.

Saturday 22 — **"Scots Mob Mrs T"** An 'astonished' Mrs Thatcher got a rousing reception in Edinburgh when she made her first major public appearance since being confirmed as Conservative Party leader.

Sunday 23 — **"Disappearing Gold"** Gold coins valued at £150,000 are missing after 10 cartons containing 500 gold pieces each, were loaded on to an aircraft in London, but only six arrived in Toronto. Canadian and British police are investigating.

Monday 24 — **"Recycling Scheme"** Councils with wastepaper schemes have been criticised for using indestructible polythene bags. A campaign is to be launched to encourage the use of re-cycled paper sacks for refuse collections.

Tuesday 25 — **"Major Oil Strike"** Conoco have confirmed a major North Sea oil discovery, proving that the huge Norwegian Statfjord field extends into British waters. The Norwegian and British governments will now have to meet to decide how best to develop the field.

HERE IN BRITAIN
"End of 'Down Your Way'"

'Down Your Way', the BBC radio programme, which in 28 years has visited most parts of Britain in search of interesting personalities and their favourite music, is to disappear as part of the corporation's cutbacks.
Brian Johnson who became the programme's presenter on the death of Franklin Engelmann, has been named this week as a member of the popular 'Twenty Questions' panel. The Down Your Way team travelled a good deal in making the broadcasts and it is believed that the rising cost of travel and accommodation has been a big consideration.

AROUND THE WORLD
"Nuclear Hell"

Hidden in Semipalatinsk, NE Kazakhstan, lies a nuclear hell, pockmarked with craters, abandoned bunkers and an atomic lake known as 'The Polygon'. This was a primary testing site for Russian nuclear weapons, with facilities built using gulag labour.
Over 400 nuclear bombs were detonated here with no regard for the local people or environment. Russia falsely claimed the vast 18,000 km² steppe was 'uninhabited', and details of the area were erased from maps for decades. Residents of the surrounding area have been affected by the radiation.

Fair Weather Vanes

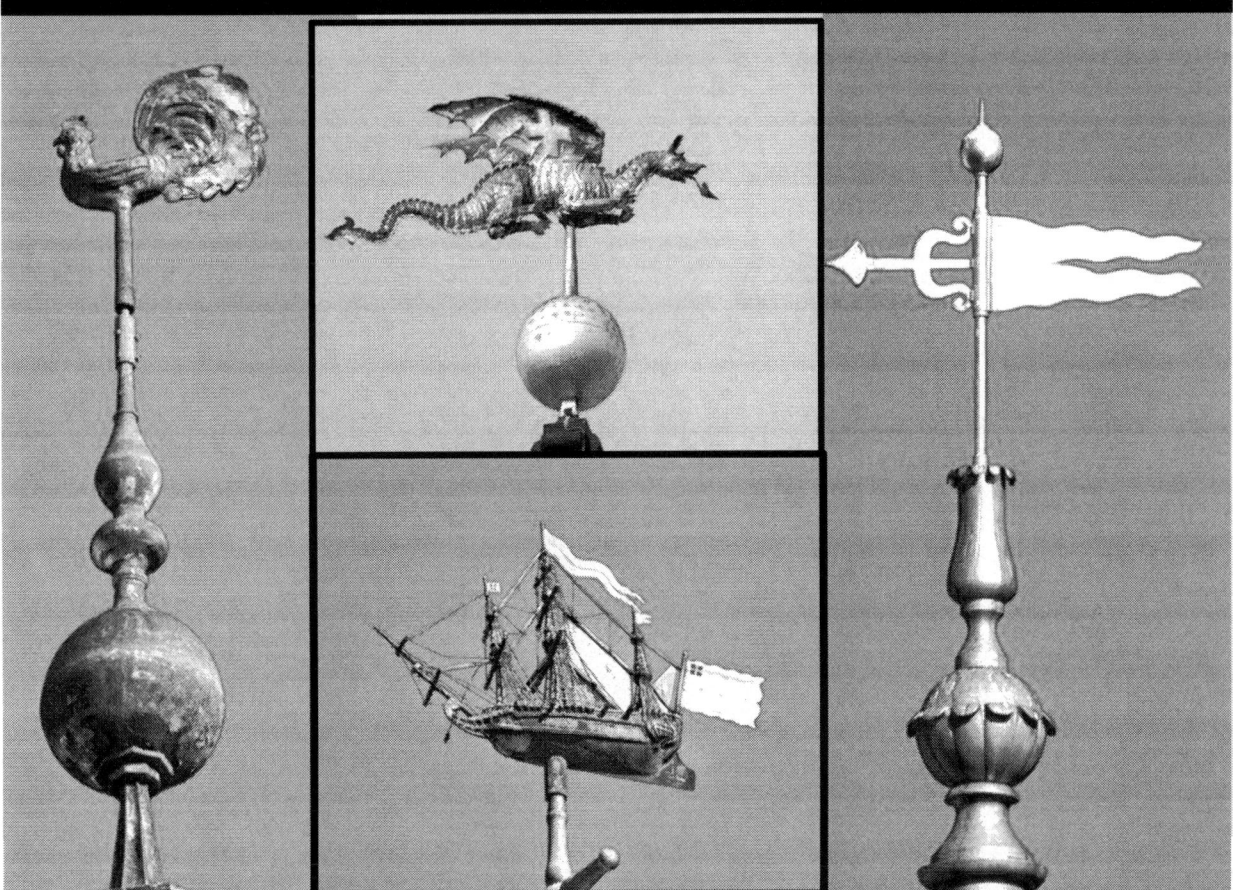

Many of the weather vanes in London are regularity cleaned and oiled in order to preserve their role in the history of the city. The capital still has many weather vanes, but most are plain arrows on church steeples, usually with a rather wide vane (or banner) as the tail to catch the wind. Some churches' vanes carry the emblem of the saint to whom they are dedicated, just as St. Peter-upon-Cornhill has keys as its design.

The tiny City church of St. Ethelburga in Bishopsgate has one of London's few remaining weathercocks, the cock itself forming the whole of one side of the vane, the other side being a banner with the date 1675. In Bishopsgate, above St. Helen's Place, the weather vane is in the form of a beaver and above the Worshipful Company of Leather sellers there is a fine antlered head. In Threadneedle Street, where the 'Old Lady' has no weather vane, is one of the City's most imposing, the giant grasshopper on the Royal Exchange. The weather vane of St. Michael, Queenhithe, a City church demolished in the last century, is now on a building near the site of the church and is in the form of a sailing ship. In former times its hull was reputed to hold a bushel of grain in token of the trade in corn carried on at Queenhithe.

Another ship in full sail can be seen on a building near London Bridge and close beside it, is a weather vane that takes the form of a multi-shafted arrow with a single head. From London Bridge you can see the huge fish that make the vanes for Billingsgate Market. Leadenhall Market has smaller twin cock pheasants. The Tower of London has many banners that turn 'with the wind, and the unattractive outposts of Cannon Street station on each of which is a plain arrow type of weather vane that has become a favourite roosting-place for starlings.

Feb 26th - March 4th 1975

IN THE NEWS

Wednesday 26 — "**Prince in TV**" Prince Charles is working on six programmes for a BBC television series on anthropology. As Patron of the Royal Anthropological Institute, he will be involved both in production and on location.

Thursday 27 — "**Moorgate Crash**" At least 29 people were killed and more than 70 injured when a rush-hour underground train crashed into the buffers at Moorgate station, in the City of London. It is the worst accident in the city's Underground history.

Friday 28 — "**Headlamps On**" The Minister for Transport, put regulations before Parliament which will compel motorists to switch on head lamps or fog lamps when daytime visibility is poor, through smoke, fog, heavy rain, spray or snow.

Sat March 1 — "**VAT Bullies**" The Government has ordered 'a thorough investigation' of an incident at Selby, Yorkshire, where a woman whose shop had been searched for nearly five hours without a warrant, said VAT inspectors used 'high-handed bullying and intimidation'.

Sunday 2 — "**Food Poisoning Rise**" Reinforced by a further outbreak of salmonella and paratyphoid infections in Keswick, public health specialists and veterinarians are pressing for urgent controls to curb the spread of these virulent bacteria from animals to humans.

Monday 3 — "**Dockers Out Again**" London dockers voted to continue their strike, which began on Thursday night and has brought almost the entire port to a standstill. About 9,000 men are involved and 19 ships in the port are idle.

Tuesday 4 — "**Refuse Tips Risk**" Uncollected refuse piling up in Glasgow city centre at the rate of a thousand tons a day, has become a serious potential threat to health. The unofficial stoppage by drivers demanding £5 a week more is seven weeks old.

HERE IN BRITAIN

"Award for the Cheshires"

Group Captain Leonard Cheshire, VC, and his wife Susan, have been given the Humanitarian Award from Variety Clubs International, in recognition of their work for sick, disabled, and homeless children.
Cheshire and his wife, Sue Ryder, founded the Cheshire Homes in 1948 and now the charity helps disabled people globally. The charity initially provided shelter to homeless and disabled veterans and became a network of 60 homes in England with more in 20 other countries. Today, the organisation supports over 20,000 disabled people worldwide.

AROUND THE WORLD

"Transplant on TV"

The first televised kidney transplant was shown on American NBC's popular "Today Show." Dr. Kountz *performed the operation live* on air intentionally to raise awareness of the plight of patients awaiting transplants. Afterwards over 20,000 people called in to the programme's switchboard offering to donate their kidneys.
The successful operation was made possible by the use of immunosuppressive drugs he helped to develop. To preserve kidneys for up to 50 hours, he invented the "Belzer kidney perfusion machine".

Saint David's Day

On the 1st March, the Countess of Anglesey was guest speaker at the annual St David's Day dinner in London, and the day was celebrated all across Wales with church services and traditional festivities. Daffodils and leeks are worn, traditional 'cawl' – a meat and vegetable soup- is eaten, and in some town, women wear their traditional dress with the unique tall black hat.

Daffodils lined the high altar in St David's Cathedral Pembrokeshire. This most revered building in Wales is home to the oldest See in Britain, having had 23 more bishops than Canterbury, with records dating back to as early as 1180. Although the original Cathedral is from the 12th Century, the current is 'at least the fourth on the site' and clergymen spoke of earthquakes and destruction that saw the symbolic rebuilding of the holy building over the following millennium.

The most holy figure in Welsh history lends his namesake to this smallest city in Britain, and also one of the earliest, first given its city status in the 12th Century. St David himself, or Dewi Sant in Welsh, was likely born circa the 6th Century, a preacher who became the definitive voice of the early Welsh church. Throughout his life, he spread the Christian mission, founding churches and monasteries all across Wales. A visit to Glastonbury at the end of his life saw him donate a large alter embedded with a great sapphire, a jewel which was stolen over 1,000 years later.

His last words to his followers came from a sermon: *'Be joyful, keep the faith, and do the little things that you have heard and seen me do.'* The phrase 'Gwnewch y pethau bychain' - 'Do the little things' - is still well-known in Wales.

March 5th - 11th 1975

IN THE NEWS

Wednesday 5 — "Silent Star" Eighty-six-year-old Charlie Chaplin, in a wheelchair, remained silent as he received a knighthood from the Queen. Afterwards he admitted, 'I was dumbfounded; I could not talk,' before being driven away in his Bentley

Thursday 6 — "Flood Prevention" Civil engineers will be able to design flood protection schemes now, thanks to research work by a team set up five years ago by the Government to investigate ways of forecasting sporadic floods

Friday 7 — "Stolen Raphael" A message alleging that the famous portrait "La Muta" by Raphael, which was stolen on February 6, may be in London, and warning that it may be set on fire, has been received by The Times newspaper.

Saturday 8 — "Workmen Rescued" Two workmen were trapped for nine hours in clay and timber rubble after a sewer tunnel in which they were working, collapsed. A shaft was sunk 30ft under the street in Harrow to allow rescuers access to free them.

Sunday 9 — "Big Mouth!" An Irishman arrested for burglary, bragged to police about how he had smuggled cannabis from Morocco to Britain in secret compartments of motor caravans. This led to the arrest of a £1m international drug smuggling gang.

Monday 10 — "Strike Costs Jobs" The British Leyland strikers are in danger of redundancy when the strike ends as the company has lost a £2m contract from Korea.

Tuesday 11 — "Escaped Again" Twelve prisoners, who were charged with an attempted escape from the Maze prison last November, have now escaped from a courthouse at Newry. Two were recaptured, but the rest are still at large.

HERE IN BRITAIN

"No Room at the Table"

Refusing to accommodate a large party of holidaymakers resulted in a company being fined £250 for breach of the Trades Description Act. A policeman booked a holiday for nine people, at the Pontin's holiday camp in Blackpool. The brochure said that large groups of relatives and friends wishing to sit together at meals need not notify the camp.

However, it transpired that the table seating was arranged for eight persons, so the two families were sat at different tables, and Mr. Ramsbottom, the manager refused to let them sit together.

AROUND THE WORLD

"Doctor Yellow"

'Doctor Yellow' is the nickname for high-speed diagnostic trains that are used on the Bullet train lines in Japan. They have a distinctive yellow livery giving rise to the name and are fitted with electronic equipment to monitor the condition of the track and overhead cables.

Line inspections are carried out regularly at full speed, up to 270 km/h or 168 mph but because the schedule for this train is not publicised, witnessing a Doctor Yellow in operation is by pure chance. As a result, seeing one is believed to bring the viewer good luck.

Our Debt To The RNLI

Nine Lifeboat Stations mark 150 years' service this year; Appledore, Courtmacsherry, Cromer, Dun Laoghaire, Hartlepool, Howth, Newcastle Co. Down, Padstow and Skegness. And yet perhaps because lifeboatmen are characteristically modest about their work, perhaps because the service they perform makes no financial demands on the ratepayer or taxpayer, many people seem unaware of the hundreds of lives they save each year and the risks they undergo. The lifeboat is expected to be at hand when needed, like the police car, the fire engine or the ambulance. The lifeboat is expected to be on hand when needed, like police cars, fire engines or ambulances. That the Royal National Life-boat Institution is supported entirely by voluntary subscriptions probably only occurs to the average person for a few moments a year when he sees a collection box or a poster appealing for funds.

Yet in coastal towns and villages the threat of disaster at sea is more imminent, the lifeboat service is more familiar and volunteers to man the boats continue to come forward amidst the changing nature of the services they have been called on to perform in recent years. The decline of the fishing industry in many parts of the country has been accompanied by a phenomenal increase in the number of pleasure-boat owners, out in force during the main holiday months of July, August and September.

As an official put it, the institution's charter is to rescue people from the sea without distinction between nationalities or circumstances and this includes *'bloody fools'* as much as those who are victims of an Act of God. A glance at the accounts of rescues in the institution's quarterly journal will convince both the unfortunate and the foolish how great is their debt to those who uncomplainingly risk their lives to save others.

March 12th – 18th 1975

IN THE NEWS

Wednesday 12   **"Rush to Join the Militants"** The London Motorists' Association, formed six weeks ago by a businessman to campaign against the proposed £1.25 road tax on drivers in London, now has 10,000 members already.

Thursday 13   **"Wide Reforms in Equality Bill"** The Sex Discrimination Bill, possibly the most comprehensive piece of legislation of its kind in the world, has been presented to Parliament. Among its main proposals is a widening of the definition of sex discrimination to include what is called unintentional discrimination.

Friday 14   **"Airlines Want More Concordes"** British and French aircraft industries are pressing for six more Concorde supersonic airliners in addition to the 16 already authorised.

Saturday 15   **"Rush to Beat the Post"** The Post Office handled piles of extra mail today as people rushed to beat the newly introduced 7p first-class letter postage rate. Postage charges have risen seven times since 1937.

Sunday 16   **"Alf's Not a Folk Hero After All"** The central character in the controversial BBC TV series, Till Death Us Do Part, Alf Garnett, holds extreme authoritarian views, is racially prejudiced and displays religious bigotry. The annual review of audiences has found, very luckily, that he has had little, if any, direct effect on the relevant attitudes of viewers.

Monday 17   **"Mini Price Increase"** Price increases by British Leyland were introduced, increasing the cost of a new Mini car by £94 to a new total of £1,184.

Tuesday 18   **"NHS Staff Object"** Catering and cleaning staff at Westminster Hospital are working to rule, depriving their patients of 'in between meals' cups of tea and treats, as they object to private patients being admitted and to volunteers, including consultants, changing beds and cleaning in the private ward.

HERE IN BRITAIN

"Trudeau in Town"

Mr Pierre Trudeau, the Canadian Prime Minister, inspected a guard of honour of the Honourable Artillery Company at Guildhall before he received the Freedom of the City of London, one of the oldest surviving traditional ceremonies still in existence, and an honour which is only open to British and Commonwealth citizens.

There are a number of rights associated with freemen including the right to drive sheep and cattle over London Bridge and carry a naked sword in public.

AROUND THE WORLD

"A Glorious Career"

The outstandingly successful American spacecraft, Mariner 10, left Mercury, having completed its last mission successfully, passing a mere 198 miles above the surface of the planet. This was its third visit to Mercury since its launch in November 1973.

On its way out it passed close to Venus and took many pictures and measurements, before being accelerated into an orbit around the Sun. The pictures were transmitted to Canberra, Australia. Mariner 10 has now 'run out of gas' and will be abandoned.

Summer? What Summer?

This year British Summer Time began at 2 am on Sunday, March 16th when clocks went forward an hour and snow and icy conditions affected the North, Midlands and East Anglia. Snow fell on Humberside, and parts of Lincolnshire and South Yorkshire. Overnight rain turned to ice in other areas and made driving conditions hazardous. There were even snow flurries in central London yesterday afternoon and scattered snow showers in some of the Home Counties.

British Summer Time was established by an act of parliament in 1916, following a campaign against the waste of working time on summer mornings. It was then adopted in the rest of the European countries involved in WW1. The practice involved putting clocks forward by one hour in Spring, so that mornings had one hour less daylight, and evenings one hour more. Clocks were then put back one hour on the last Sunday in October and summertime ended. The length of the actual day did not alter but sunrise and sunset appeared to be an hour later. During WWII, in order to increase productivity in industry and agriculture, Britain used British Double Summertime, meaning that clocks were put forward by two hours during the summer, and in winter they were put back only one hour. From 1901-1936 King Edward VII operated a daylight-saving system at Sandringham because he loved hunting in winter. Therefore, all the clocks on the Norfolk estate were put forward by 30 minutes!

In 1959 many wanted a permanent change to clocks going forward by one hour, and in 1966 the government introduced the British Standard Time Experiment for a year, with clocks being one hour ahead for 12 months, before reverting to normal again.

March 19th – 25th 1975

IN THE NEWS

Wednesday 19 — **"Stay in Europe"** The Government has decided to recommend that Britain should stay within the European Economic Community. The Cabinet vote was 16-7 in favour, and most of those voting against, later signed a declaration welcoming a referendum and inviting 'our fellow citizens to join us' in the campaign for withdrawal.

Thursday 20 — **"Teacher Redundancies"** Richmond on Thames Council have decided to cut £1m from the education budget and make 200 teachers redundant, after talks with national leaders of teaching unions.

Friday 21 — **"Christies Con"** Three men bid successfully for 12 auction lots of diamonds and other precious stone jewellery worth £224,010 at Christies. They then secured the lots with 'forged cash receipts.' Scotland Yard is investigating this 'brazen confidence trick'.

Saturday 22 — **"College Closures"** Nearly a fifth of teacher training colleges in England and Wales will close due to cuts in the teacher training targets. The number of students training will be more than halved over the next few years, from the present 108,000 to 60,000.

Sunday 23 — **"Sell by Dates"** Legislation is to be introduced to require food processors and shopkeepers to show, on packets of pre-packed foods, the dates by which they should be sold. White sugar, fresh fruit and vegetables, and frozen products will be exempt.

Monday 24 — **"Duke's Plane Diverted"** The turbojet of the Queen's Flight carrying the Duke of Edinburgh home from his Caribbean tour developed engine trouble and was forced to make two unscheduled landings, in North Carolina and later in Ontario.

Tuesday 25 — **"Fishing Blockade"** Two hundred miles of coastline, from Blyth, Sunderland and Hartlepool in the Northeast down to Whitby and Scarborough on the Yorkshire coast, was blockaded by fishermen protesting against cheap fish imports.

HERE IN BRITAIN

"Patriots Ready"

Members of GB 75, a patriotic volunteer organisation, now have a new director, who is an engineer with much practical experience in the power industry. Prominent businessmen and professionals were sent discussion papers outlining contingency plans for running vital public utilities in the event of a general strike.

The organisation is anxious to emphasize that it is not a private army and is now concentrating all its activities to equip its members to take over the power stations if called on by the Government to do so.

AROUND THE WORLD

"King Faisal Assassinated"

Saudi Arabia's King Faisal who implemented a policy of modernisation and reform, was shot at point blank range by his nephew this week. Popular with his subjects, Faisal was fiercely pro-Palestine and protested against the support that Israel received from the West.

However, his advocacy of limiting the power of Islamic religious officials, was not liked by many traditionalists, and his introduction of national TV was considered a step too far by many, including the son of his half-brother who was convicted of regicide and beheaded in Riyadh.

Spring Crops

Daffodils in the Scilly Isles (main). A rhubarb shed in Yorkshire (inset).

The Scilly Isles benefit from warmer, milder, spring weather than the rest of Britain, lying in the centre of the Gulf Stream, 28 miles from Land's End. Flower growing has been a mainstay of the islands' economy for centuries, as the growing conditions are excellent with fields sheltered from winds by high hedges. Daffodils can survive and thrive in cooler conditions, but the smaller, scented narcissi breeds need a little more warmth. These are grown commercially on four of the five inhabited islands, keeping up the long-held island tradition of producing high quality and beautifully scented flowers that arrive in our shops each early spring.

Another early crop hails from another island to the south of our shores - the Jersey Royal potato which has been grown since 1878, when a farmer cut two huge potatoes into small pieces which he planted on a côtil (steep sloping field), and several months later harvested a large early crop of small, kidney shaped potatoes. Seaweed from local beaches, known as vraic, is still used as fertiliser, and the crops are hand-lifted as the côtils are too steep for harvesting machinery. Jersey royals are still at their best simply boiled and seasoned with butter and salt.

450 miles north east, Leeds, Wakefield and Bradford grow early rhubarb. Almost all the rhubarb eaten in Britain is actually grown there. Forcing rhubarb (producing a crop outside its natural season) was discovered in 1817, when roots, covered over winter, produced tastier and more tender new shoots earlier than normal. The plant is grown in low, rhubarb 'sheds' which have a chimney at one end where the cheap, local, coal is burnt to provide heat and this produces a very early crop. A large industry has developed, and in spring, special trains leave Yorkshire nightly to ship large quantities of rhubarb down to Covent Garden Market.

March 26th – April 1st 1975

IN THE NEWS

Wednesday 26   "**No Daily Mirror**" Publication of the Daily Mirror was suspended after 1,750 warehouse staff were dismissed, following an unofficial walk-out which caused the loss of nearly half the paper's run of 3,200,000 copies.

Thursday 27   "**Happy Postmen**" Britain's 200,000 Post Office workers have voted overwhelmingly to accept a new pay deal that provides postmen with a £7.50 basic wage increase, giving them a new basic rate of £38.50 a week.

Friday 28   "**New Safety Zones**" Ten new safety zones have been created around oil and gas installations in the North Sea. Shipping of all nationalities cannot approach within 500 metres of production platforms, except in emergencies or to provide services.

Saturday 29   "**North Wind Doth Blow**" Ice and snow falls of up to 6" marked the beginning of the Easter weekend, as an Arctic air stream swept south through the country. Heathrow airport was closed for two hours to allow snow clearing to take place.

Sunday 30   "**NHS in Trouble**" Mrs Castle, the Social Services Minister, bluntly rejected the diagnosis presented to her by the House of Commons Expenditure Committee that the NHS was 'grinding to a halt'. She did agree it needs more money.

Monday 31   "**Guernsey Limits Settlers**" Guernsey's Parliament decided to restrict the right of outsiders to live on the island. In future they will need a special residency license before they can settle there.

Tuesday 1 April "**Combating Illiteracy**" A group of traditional academics have presented a 'Black Paper' saying progressive education is not working. Literacy is declining, with half the adult illiterates being below the age of 25. A new seven plus exam to get all normal children reading before they can move on to junior school, is proposed.

HERE IN BRITAIN

"Pride of Belgium"

Two racing pigeons from Belgium are now living in Britain and it is expected that their progeny will add a new dimension to the already excellent, British racing pigeon. Mr Louis Massarella paid 6,500 Euros to get them to the pigeon lofts on his farm in Leicestershire.

Mr Massarella, a self-made millionaire from farming and ice-cream production, has kept pigeons since he was nine, when they cost him a few pence from the Kirby Muxloe market.

AROUND THE WORLD

"Luxury Liners to Go"

The Italian Government and trade unions have agreed on a drastic economy plan for Italy's merchant marine. In all, 15 luxury liners will be taken out of service over the next three years and replaced with nearly 100 new freighters.

Only five liners will survive the drastic cuts, the Marconi, the Galilei, the Rossini, the Vittoria and the Ausonia. The unions agreed to the plan only after the Government pledged not to make seamen redundant in the process.

APRIL FOOL

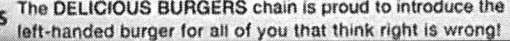

Celebrating April 1st is not a modern custom, as it dates back to the 16th century when Catholic countries in Europe switched from the old Julian calendar, where New Year began with the Spring Equinox around April 1st, to the Gregorian calendar with the New Year celebrated on 1st January. People who continued to celebrate the New Year at the start of April were called 'April fools'.

In the Middle Ages it became accepted to play pranks on people on that day. It is recorded that in 1698, several people were tricked into going to the Tower of London to see the lions being washed! In Britain, a trick is revealed by shouting "April fool!" at the recipient, but only until noon, after which time it is no longer acceptable, in fact, after midday, the trickster becomes the fool! In Scotland the day is called Gowkie Day, for the gowk, or cuckoo, a symbol of the fool.

The custom isn't unique to our country. Some people celebrate it just as a special day, with family and friends and special foods. But for many it is a day for superstition, playing tricks or telling lies. In Iran, it is called 'Dorugh-e Sizdah' which translates as "getting rid of 13," celebrated on the thirteenth day of the Persian New Year. In France, Belgium and Italy, paper fish are stuck to people's backs, making them 'Poisson d'Avril' or April fish. In Spain some towns have a big food fight, while in Germany they merely resort to shouting April! April! at each other, rather like a verbal 'thumbing your nose'. In Poland, serious activities are usually avoided as every word spoken could be untrue. Back in 1683 a treaty was actually backdated to March 31st to avoid any doubt that it was genuine.

April 2nd – 8th 1975

IN THE NEWS

Wednesday 2 — **"Great Train Robbers Freed"** Two members of the gang that stole £2.6m in the mail train robbery 12 years ago, James White and 'Buster' Edwards, have been released after serving roughly half their sentences. One robber, Ronald Biggs, is still at large in Brazil.

Thursday 3 — **"Fish Prices Up"** Some retail fish prices have risen by half because of the inshore fishermen's blockade of English and Scottish ports. Varieties such as whiting, herring and mackerel may soon become scarce.

Friday 4 — **"Resistance to Diets"** An article in 'The Lancet' explains, for the first time, how scientists have proved that prolonged dieting can lead to a drop in the body's need for food meaning that a standard reducing diet no longer has any effect.

Saturday 5 — **"Non-Runner"** The owner of Aintree Racecourse paid £14,000 for 'Wolverhampton', stablemate of 'Red Rum', the favourite, to race him in today's Grand National. However, the horse died after exercising on the beach at Southport yesterday.

Sunday 6 — **"Britons to Leave"** Britons have been advised to evacuate South Vietnam immediately, after several West European embassies reached the conclusion that Saigon will inevitably fall into communist hands.

Monday 7 — **"Calling Bright Sparks"** Mensa, the 'club for people with a high IQ, published a booklet describing its purpose and the measurement of intelligence on which admission depends, following an unprecedented flood of applications. 16,000 inquiries have been received in the first 10 weeks of the year.

Tuesday 8 — **"Monks Business"** The monastery on Caldey Island in Wales is taking delivery of a £3,000 electronic accounting machine, as their business ventures are now too complex and extensive for the old bookkeeping system.

HERE IN BRITAIN

"Violence on the Rise"

After more than 6,000 cases of classroom violence and disruption were reported during a single school term a former leader of the National Union of Teachers said, 'It does teachers no good to give the public the impression that we walk in fear and trembling of seven-year-old babies or 15-year-old youngsters. However, disruptive behaviour was increasing. It began in homes where parents thought it modern to let children do as they pleased. Such 'trendiness' was greatly despised by the children themselves.'

AROUND THE WORLD

"Microsoft Born"

A feature in 'Popular Electronics' inspired childhood friends Bill Gates and Paul Allen to say to the computer company MITS, that they could program a BASIC (Beginners' All-purpose Symbolic Instruction Code) interpreter for the Altair 8800 which they successfully demonstrated in Albuquerque, New Mexico, in March 1975.

On April 4th Gates and Allen then established their own company, Microsoft, which is short for micro-computer software, now the world's leading PC operating systems business.

Costly Doll's Houses

As early as 1920 the Government decided to hold a British Empire Exhibition as there was a sense that other powers were challenging Britain on the world stage. It was opened at Wembley Park in April 1974 and when the Exhibition ended in April 1975, although over 27 million visitors passed through the turnstiles, the endeavour had made a loss. There were four main Palaces, Engineering, Industry, The Arts, and Government, as well as over 50 Pavilions housing the exhibits of individual nations and kiosks for major companies from within those countries.

One of the most popular exhibits within the Palace of The Arts, attracting over 1.6 million visitors was a doll's house made to a scale of 1:12 (one inch to one foot), over three feet tall, and containing models of products made by well-known companies of the time, many of which are 1/12th sized replicas of items in Windsor Castle. It was made for Queen Mary, wife of King George V and later, the doll's house was put on display at Windsor Castle to raise funds for the Queen's charities.

The house itself was designed by Sir Edward Lutyens, with fully working lighting and plumbing, including a flushing toilet. The furnishings and carpets are faithfully reproduced in designs that were fashionable in the royal houses at the time and the library is filled with miniature books and the walls adorned with paintings. Even the bottles in the wine cellar are filled with the appropriate wines and spirits, and the wheels of motor vehicles were properly spoked. There is a hidden garden which is revealed only when a vast drawer is pulled out from beneath the main building.

April 9th – 15th 1975

IN THE NEWS

Wednesday 9 — **"Cairngorms Blizzard"** Severe blizzards and gale force winds swept the Cairngorms, keeping skiers off the slopes, while rescuers searched the area for a missing mountaineer.

Thursday 10 — **"The North South Divide"** The call for the introduction of regional budgets is being strongly supported by the Northern Planning Council, where there is a strong feeling that the industrial areas of the North need a bigger share of national resources.

Friday 11 — **"Advertising Curbs"** A code for tighter controls over cigarette advertising is to be introduced. It will stop advertisements which portray smoking as connected with health, bravery, and success.

Saturday 12 — **"Live Exports"** Regulations covering the live export of animals are to be tightened by the Ministry of Agriculture, Fisheries and Food, due to allegations of cruelty to sheep exported to France.

Sunday 13 — **"Leap of Faith"** A Camberwell man decided to test his faith in God the day after his marriage, by stepping off the balcony of his thirteenth floor flat, in the belief that we would not be killed. He used to carry a sandwich board displaying religious texts.

Monday 14 — **"Back to Work"** Glasgow dustcart drivers have ended their three-month unofficial strike and returned to work after all troops were withdrawn from the city. The strike leaders said the drivers had *'been starved back to work'*.

Tuesday 15 — **"Rag Bag of Measures"** In Mr Healey's Budget, the basic and higher rates of income tax rose by 2 per cent; the married allowance goes to £955 and the single allowance £675 and a new scheme of family allowances, or child benefits, for *all* children, not just the first as at present, will be proposed.

HERE IN BRITAIN
"Rough, Tough, Budget"

Denis Healey posed for newspaper photographers on the steps of No.11 Downing Street, with the red leather dispatch box containing his speech. He delivered a *"rough, tough"* Spring budget, raising taxes and cutting spending, with higher duty on alcohol, cigarettes and bingo.

The new leader of the opposition, Margaret Thatcher, called it a genuine socialist budget, consisting of *"equal shares of misery for all"*. Police making a Budget Day check on a suspicious object on a windowsill overlooking 11, Downing Street, found it was someone's packed lunch!

AROUND THE WORLD
"Italians in Colour"

A political debate has broken out over whether expensive colour television sets should be advertised in the country's worst economic crisis since WWII. The Deputy Prime Minister, reasoned, *"How can we continue to ask Italians to make all kinds of sacrifices and then encourage them to buy this extremely expensive luxury?"*

Two years ago, discussions on colour televisions were shelved to discourage unnecessary spending, but industrialists are now anxious to get the electronics sector, which has suffered heavily because of the delay, back on its feet.

THE PILGRIM TRUST

The Pilgrim Trust's first project was the shoring up of Durham Cathedral.

The Savernake Horn, mentioned in records since 1586, a hunting horn carved from an elephant's tusk, has been acquired from the 8th Marquess of Aylesbury, the hereditary warden of Savernake Forest, for the British Museum at a cost of £250,000. Contributions had come from the Pilgrim Trust.

The Pilgrim Trust was established in 1930 by Edward Harkness, an American philanthropist, whose family traced its roots to Dumfriesshire. He had a lifelong love of Great Britain and after our contribution to the First World War, donated £2 million to create the Trust. This large gift captured the country's imagination, and the King and Queen received him and his wife at Buckingham Palace. In 1931, the Trust's first grant of £25,000 went to Durham Castle, which with shifting foundations, was in urgent need of work to save the building from sliding into the River Wear. But much of their early work focused on the high levels of unemployment in the country and gave individuals employment and volunteering opportunities. They commissioned a report - 'Men Without Work', which explored the unemployed across six towns, which was a significant piece of research. At the outbreak of WWII, an ambitious scheme, the brainchild of Sir Kenneth Clark, was set up to employ artists on the home front. The result is a collection of more than 1,500 watercolours and drawings that make up a fascinating record of British lives and landscapes at what was a time of great imminent change from a time of history into the modern world.

Today they actively pursue the preservation and restoration of the nation's heritage of beautiful things, by making grants to other charities and public bodies in the fields of preservation and scholarship and social welfare.

April 16th – 22nd 1975

IN THE NEWS

Wednesday 16   "**Discreet Warning**" A discreet Home Office circular explaining how the British people will be told of an imminent nuclear war, and kept informed during an attack, has been sent to local authorities and emergency services. However, *'the possibility of the time scale being much shorter than the planning assumption cannot be entirely discounted.'*

Thursday 17   "**A New Star**" A new type of star has been discovered by a group of British astronomers from universities in London and Birmingham. It was discovered using the British satellite known as 'Ariel-S'.

Friday 18   "**Bosworth Field**" The battlefield site in Leicestershire, has been short-listed for this year's conservation awards with derelict farm buildings becoming an education facility.

Saturday 19   "**Ice Bound Prince**" The Prince of Wales has begun an 11-day Canadian visit, most of which will be in the Arctic. At Frobisher Bay, he will take a 12-mile dog-sled ride and see the lighting of a gas flare at a natural gas well.

Sunday 20   "**Fighting Water Pollution**" Awards for Industry have been given to five British and two international companies for schemes to reduce water pollution. The gold medal was won by the Scottish Distillers Company.

Monday 21   "**Call for Compulsory Radios**" The loss of the Compass Rose III, an oil survey vessel, in a North Sea storm and the drowning of her crew of 18, has brought a call for stricter radio safety regulations and a compulsory coastguard reporting system for all ships.

Tuesday 22   "**Just in Time**" Mr Edward Heath's new £55,000 yacht, Morning Cloud, has been finished ahead of schedule and will not be subject to the 'doubled' value-added tax of 25% on 'luxury goods', which becomes operational on May 1.

HERE IN BRITAIN

"Learning at Leisure"

A series of cassettes are being produced which aims to be the first comprehensive selection of spoken-word cassettes in Britain. They are already hugely popular in America where they sell almost as well as music cassettes, and it is hoped they will prove to be the same in this country.

A range of subjects including drama, driving, golf, history, cooking and music will be available, with sound by writers, actors and musicians. The cassettes will have a running time of about an hour, and each will cost £2.95.

AROUND THE WORLD

"A Glorious Bicentennial"

It is difficult to pinpoint exactly where and when the American Revolution began. Boston had its tea party, and Philadelphia its Continental Congress. But the shot heard around the world was fired 200 years ago, when Paul Revere rode through, shouting *"The British are coming!"* and the Redcoats marched on Concord and Lexington.

President Ford's bicentennial speech stressed the a restoration of traditional values, in his nostalgic reading of the American past.

THE EAGLE

25 years ago this month, the most famous of Marcus Morris's publications, 'The Eagle' comic went on sale. Born in Preston, Lancashire the son of a clergyman, Morris became an Anglican Priest in 1940 and from the beginning, he published Christian magazines for his younger parishioners, illustrated by Frank Hampson. He was part of a group of editors who formed the Society of Christian Publicity, and wrote an article entitled "Comics that bring Horror into the Nursery", decrying the violence of American crime and horror comics. He was impressed by the high standard of artwork but disgusted by their content. Realising a market existed for a children's comic featuring cartoon action stories but conveying Christian standards and morals, he and Hampson produced The Eagle.

The comic was enormously successful, the first issue selling 900,000 copies. The full colour cover featured the iconic *"Dan Dare, Pilot of The Future"*, created by Hampson, which was the UK's first science-fiction comic strip of any significance. Other popular stories included *"Riders of the Range"* and *"PC. 49"*. Eagle also contained news, sport sections, and educational cutaway diagrams of sophisticated machinery, the first of which, detailed the inner workings of the British Rail 18000 locomotive.

A member's club was created, and a range of related merchandise licensed for sale. The comic was heavily publicised before its release; copies were mailed direct to several hundred thousand people who worked with children, and a "Hunt the Eagle" scheme was launched, whereby large papier-mâché golden eagles were set on top of several Humber Hawk cars, and toured across Britain. Those who spotted an eagle were offered tokens worth 3d which could be exchanged for a free copy.

April 23rd – 29th 1975

IN THE NEWS

Wednesday 23 — **"Thanksgiving Service"** The Queen attended a service of thanksgiving on St. George's Day with members of the Royal Family at St George's Chapel, Windsor, to celebrate the 500th Anniversary of its construction.

Thursday 24 — **"It Fell off the Back of a Lorry"** A lorry carrying a sculpture by Henry Moore overturned on the Winchester by-pass, and heavy lifting gear had to be used to raise it from the road. The sculpture is undamaged and currently awaiting collection from the garage, to continue its journey to Geneva.

Friday 25 — **"High Price to Pay"** The annual cost of running the average family car has risen by nearly £240 in the past year, which for many motorists is more than the mortgage repayments on his house.

Saturday 26 — **"Middle Class Image"** Public libraries have achieved a middle-class image, which puts off a large part of the population from using them. The problem and causes are being investigated by a working party.

Sunday 27 — **"Treasure Trove"** Kent Police took part in a midnight digging treasure hunt and found £200,000 cash, and jewellery worth £40,000 stolen from the Bank of America in Mayfair.

Monday 28 — **"A Huge Mistake"** The Post Office Corporation is having to admit it has made a huge error so instead of the predicted £50m deficit for the current financial year, it estimates that its overall loss could be as high as £300m, and prices will have to rise.

Tuesday 29 — **"Not Screening For All"** A working party have recommended that a 'national breast cancer screening service' is unjustified. However, the Health Minister has accepted advice to operate trials to establish an 'optimum level of service'.

HERE IN BRITAIN

"Abundant Oyster Harvest"

Loch Melfort, in Argyll, is about to yield its first harvest of 500,000 farmed oysters. Forty feet down in the clear, fish-rich waters, divers will collect the batches of marketable oysters bound for tables in Europe, Scandinavia and Russia. By next year the group of sea-farmers expect to have 1,250,000 Pacific oysters, which they have reared from pinhead size, ready for the market.

A company, Western Aquaculture, is one of the sea-farming organisations that the Government has helped to promote through the Highlands and Islands Development Board, leading to Argyll's growing significance.

AROUND THE WORLD

"All Things Being Equal"

Italy's Parliament has approved legislation which has been awaiting approval for 10 years and which brings family affairs into line with the requirements of the 1948 Constitution.

The wife may keep her maiden name, and all goods and income accruing after the marriage are the property of both. The institution of the dowry is abolished. The law abolishes the husband's exclusive right to decide where the family lives, and any children born out of wedlock will have the same rights as legitimate ones.

The RAF - Pink's War

> O Wingy Pink! O Wingy Pink!
> What awful things your brain does think!
> This awful slush, these sobs and sighs,
> Brings tears to the eyes of them what flies!
>
> When naughty words like "hell" and "blazes"
> Flash before their spellbound gazes,
> They think how he'll laugh—that local Khan
> When he reads Pinky's Piece in Waziristan!
>
> —Wing Commander R.C.M. Pink, 1925

A poem written by Wing Commander Pink (top) and a Bristol F.2B fighter, one of the types of aircraft used in Pink's War.

The RAF was formed just three years and eight months into WWI, by amalgamating the Royal Flying Corps and the Royal Naval Air Service. When the war of 1914 started, the aeroplane was a new and untried weapon, but it rapidly developed as both a weapon of offence and defence. When the allies mounted their counter-offensive in 1918, the RAF was able to concentrate 1,290 first-line aircraft against its opponents' 340, and, enjoying this air superiority, was able to disrupt the Germans' communications and harass their troops by low flying attacks. When the Armistice came, the RAF was the greatest air force in the world, both numerically and in quality of equipment, possessing more than 200 squadrons, 22,647 aircraft of all, 103 airships and a total strength of 291,000 officers and men.

After the war the Service shrank to a shadow of its former self but managed to keep many members possessing a pioneering spirit. *Pink's War* was an air-to-ground bombardment and strafing campaign carried out by the Royal Air Force, led by against a rebellion by mountain tribesmen in India. It was the first independent action by the RAF, and remains the only campaign named after an RAF officer. At the end of April 1925, after just over 50 days of bombing, the tribal leaders sought peace, bringing the short campaign to a close. Only two British lives and one aircraft were lost during the campaign.

At the beginning of WW2, we had far fewer planes than Germany and the country has undergone a massive drive to build Spitfires and Hurricane fighters, and Wellington, Whitley and Hampden bombers. All technically superior to the German planes, but it was, nonetheless, a dangerous situation until the Battle of Britain had been won.

April 30th – May 6th 1975

IN THE NEWS

Wednesday 30 — **"Brain Scanner"** A new form of X-ray diagnosis is to start trials at hospitals in Britain and America. The new C-scan produces a highly accurate picture of soft organ tissue including the brain, as well as the bone structure.

Thurs May 1 — **"Wild Birds Protest"** 600,000 wild birds are imported into Britain annually. An RSPB report criticises the conditions in which they are trapped and is calling for the Government to ban the trade.

Friday 2 — **"Hostel Plan for The Depraved"** A Christian organisation wants to open a hostel in London for 'victims of moral pollution'. Pornography addicts, sexual deviants and *"others involved in erotica"* would follow a course of compulsory spiritual activities.

Saturday 3 — **"Britons to Attend Soviet VE Day"** Lord Mountbatten, representing the Queen, will head a British delegation to Moscow, for a ceremony marking the 30th anniversary of the end of the war in Europe.

Sunday 4 — **"End of Charge"** A High Court judge has ruled that it is illegal to demand sewerage charges where premises are not connected to public sewers. About 900,000 households will benefit from the ruling.

Monday 5 — **"New Paper for Scotland"** The first edition of the Scottish Daily News has rolled off the press in Glasgow, watched over by Mr Wedgwood Benn, Secretary of State for Industry, and Mr Robert Maxwell, the publisher,

Tuesday 6 — **"Farmers Smash French Eggs"** Farmers in Southampton and Plymouth have protested against the import of cheaply produced French eggs and near Exeter a lorry load of French eggs was smashed up by farmers with crowbars.

HERE IN BRITAIN

"Whittington Walks"

A group of London mayors, and mayoresses, in traditional dress with their heavy gold chains, began their annual five-mile charity walk from Highgate Hill to the Mansion House by petting the statue of Dick Whittington's cat.

This commemorates the 'turning again' of Dick Whittington and his cat on Highgate Hill before Whittington became Lord Mayor of London. The Pearly King and Pearly Prince of Finsbury, who represent the famous 'pearlies', or the London Pearly Kings' and Queens' Society, one of London's oldest charities, accompanied the councillors.

AROUND THE WORLD

"Free Education"

The South African education reforms were originally designed to create a new educated Black middle class opposed to the African National Congress and other liberation movements. However, teachers have rejected the current syllabus which is inferior to White education. There is a shortage of schools in rural and township areas for Black education and while the government policy states that each community should raise a 'School Building Fund' for physically building their own schools, the subsidy is still significantly lower than that given to White schools.

The Fall Of Saigon

SURRENDER!

Saigon Yields Unconditionally; End Comes Only Hours After Last Americans Fly Out

On the 30th April, South Vietnamese President Duong Van Minh announced an unconditional surrender, asking his forces to lay down their arms. In a radio address to the Vietcong he said, "*We are here to hand over to you the power in order to avoid bloodshed,*" and appealed to them to halt all hostilities, bringing 35 years of fighting in South Vietnam to an end.

Swarms of helicopters lifted thousands of Americans and Vietnamese military and civilian personnel from Saigon in the final withdrawal from Vietnam. Twenty years of United States involvement ended in scenes of chaos as weeping Vietnamese pleaded for places in evacuation convoys and tried to force their way into the American Embassy. American Marine and civilian helicopters, flying in groups of three, plucked evacuees from the top of the embassy building and ledges of blocks of flats. The evacuation began after a Vietcong demand, agreed to by President Duong Van Minh, that all Americans leave the country within 24 hours, the withdrawal of the United States Seventh Fleet from Vietnam waters and the disarming of Saigon's army and police.

Meanwhile in the streets, looting broke out - two policemen were seen putting their weapons into a chest of drawers to be able to cart it away more easily, while small boys struggled to carry away armchairs. Helicopters were ditched wholesale into the sea in the frantic evacuation. In the first 90 minutes of the operation, 14 helicopters carrying among others, Air Vice-Marshal Nguyen Cao Ky, the former vice-president, landed on the small helicopter pad on the back of the command ship Blue Ridge, and were then dumped, after discharging their passengers, into the sea to make room for more, while rescue boats sped around the ship to fish out the helicopter pilots.

May 7th – May 13th 1975

IN THE NEWS

Wednesday 7 — **"Church Devastated"** Streatham's landmark, the 14th century St Leonard's Church, has been destroyed by fire. The flames were fanned by a strong east wind, and swept through the Nave and up the tower, destroying all the interior woodwork, the roof and the bells.

Thursday 8 — **"Channel Island Celebrations"** An exhibition opened at the Imperial War Museum to celebrate the thirtieth anniversary of the Islands' liberation from five years of German occupation during the last war.

Friday 9 — **"Mine Widows Protest"** Miners' widows on coal board pensions of only £2.38 a week, staged a protest at the Union of Mineworkers conference, that the men, who are backing a £100 a week pay claim, have ignored their plight.

Saturday 10 — **"Royal Tour of Japan"** The Imperial Family hosted a State Banquet in honour of Queen Elizabeth and the Duke of Edinburgh during their first State Visit to the Empire of Japan.

Sunday 11 — **"Marriage Of Equals"** The Church of England will introduce a marriage service in modern language which addresses the couple as equal partners, the bride acknowledging that her earnings as well as her husband's, are to be shared.

Monday 12 — **"Armed Guards at Heathrow"** King Hussain of Jordan arrived in London to tight military security at Heathrow airport amid general concern of possible terrorist activity, and a newspaper report of an assassination plot.

Tuesday 13 — **"Old Attitude"** The agriculture minister said that Britain cannot find adequate and cheap food supplies outside the EEC. The idea that Commonwealth countries would "*queue up to meet our needs if we left the Community*" revealed '*an outmoded attitude.*'

HERE IN BRITAIN

"It's Not All in the Mind"

Scientists showed how to bend spoons and other metal objects without Uri Geller's aid of supernatural powers, at the Royal Society in London. They called it, the 'mechanical memory of materials', saying many materials, particularly new alloys developed for the aerospace business, such as nickel-titanium, can be given two natural shapes. A demonstration showed a piece of wire, which at room temperature was straight, placed in a bath of warm water about 65C where it suddenly transformed to a curved shape.

AROUND THE WORLD

"Giant Hailstones in Tennessee"

During a recent storm, hail stones as large as tennis balls hit Wernerville, Tennessee. With insurance companies swamped by claims, vehicle owners face prolonged waits for coverage and repairs. Farmers affected by the hail are now evaluating the extent of damage to their crops and determining if replanting will be necessary. Hail two inches or larger in diameter is classed as 'Significant Severe Hail' which coupled with winds of 75 mph or higher, can cause considerable damage to property and severe injury to humans.

The Ice Saints

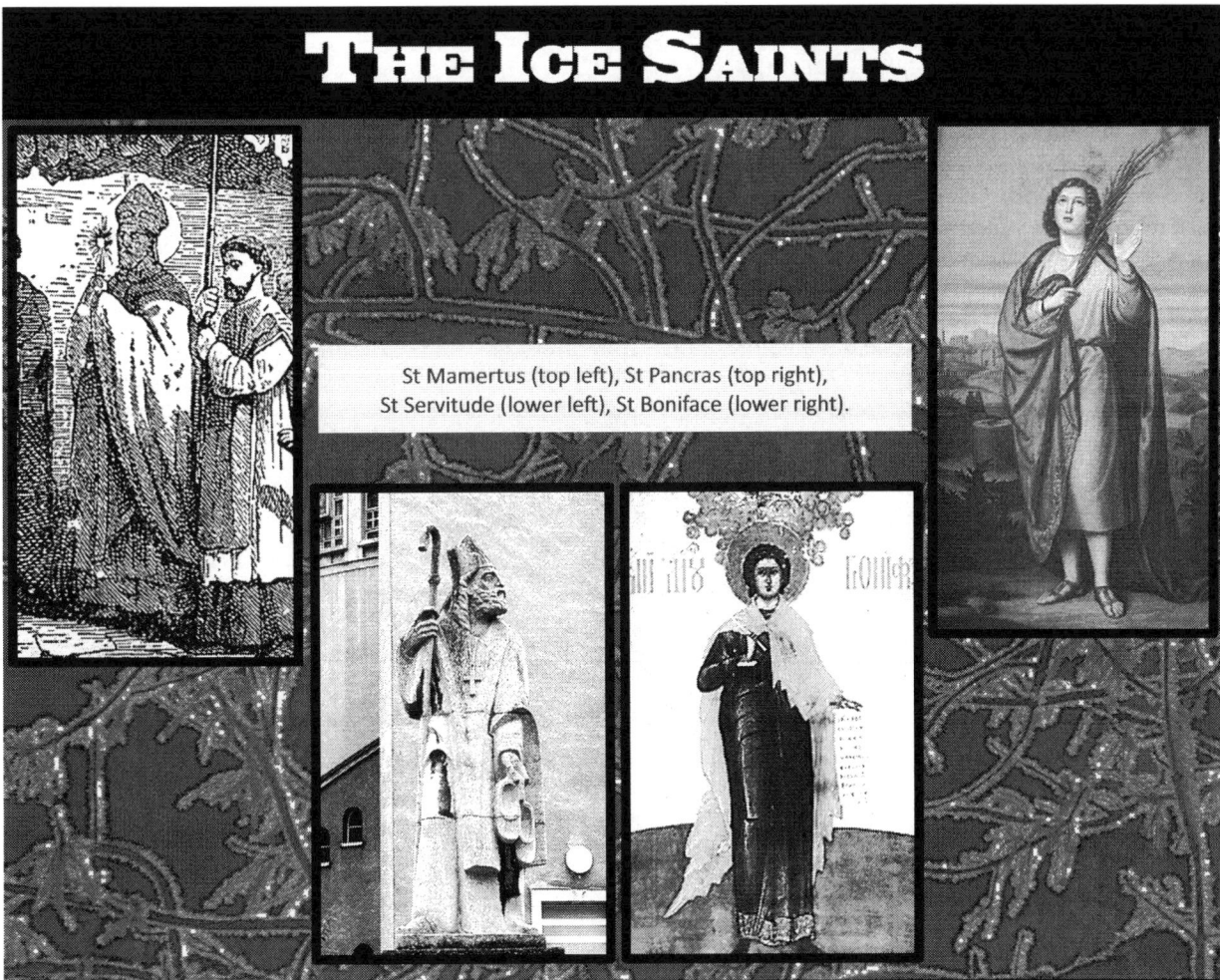

St Mamertus (top left), St Pancras (top right),
St Servitude (lower left), St Boniface (lower right).

In traditional weather lore, cold weather and late frosts in the spring is of prime importance to all gardeners and farmers, who need to protect tender shoots and buds from damage if a good crop is to be secured for later in the year. And, as with much weather phenomena, there are saints associated with it, known throughout Europe as 'The Ice Saints'. According to tradition, the feast days of St Mamertus, St Pancras, St Servatius and St Boniface on May 11 to 14, respectively, can be surprisingly cold and as a saying goes, *"He who shears his sheep before St Servatius' Day loves his wool more than his sheep."*

This alleged 'mid-May cold spell' was even investigated by some of Galileo's pupils who, indeed, recorded the occurrence of colder weather over this period from 1655-70. But in 1902 William Dines, President of the Royal Meteorological Society, debunked the myth, using modern statistical techniques to show that the legend of the Ice Saints was merely a result of selective reporting and a review of Kew Gardens data from 1941-69 showed that 13th May was, in fact, usually the warmest day of the month. Despite this, however, many gardeners across Europe will keep tender summer flowers and vegetables under glass until the Ice Saints' days have passed.

The Ice Saints are well known across Central Europe. In Poland they are known as 'The Cold Gardeners' and are followed by 'Sophia the Ice Woman' on the feast day of St. Sophia, which falls on May 15 and in Czechoslovakia they are called 'The Icy Men'. However, the saints themselves have little to do with cold weather, it just happens that their traditional feasts are celebrated in the middle of May, when the last winter cold fronts tend to pass by.

Editor's note: In the early 1900s a common phrase was "n'er cast a clout before May is out". (Don't stop wearing winter underclothes before the end of May). A reference to cold May days.

May 14th – 20th 1975

IN THE NEWS

Wednesday 14   **"430 Pay Beds to Go"** The Department of Health say that 430 pay beds will be phased out from National Health Service hospitals, with 10 per cent being cut immediately.

Thursday 15   **"Daughters as Home Helps"** The Department for Social Security has advised single women with elderly parents to register as home helps in their own homes to get financial help from councils. An estimated 310,000 unmarried girls care for elderly parents.

Friday 16   **"Birch for Muggers"** Ten robberies were witnessed in one hour at Clapham North Tube station, and calls to the police went unanswered. A staff member said, *'small fines are no answer to violence. We must take drastic measures even if it means bringing back the birch.'*

Saturday 17   **"Blood Trade"** The World Health Organization has expressed concern over the extensive trade in human blood, which is sold by the poor in underdeveloped countries for export to affluent nations.

Sunday 18   **"Radio 1 Roadshow Disaster"** 39 people received hospital treatment following a crush of fans at the Radio One Road Show in Leicestershire. The Bay City Rollers left by helicopter without performing.

Monday 19   **"Britain's Inflation"** Inflation in Britain is now worse than almost every industrialised country except Turkey, having passed 30% (by some calculations). At this rate, prices would double, and money lose half its value every two years.

Tuesday 20   **"Home Grown"** The Chelsea Flower Show, held in the grounds of the Royal Hospital, was opened for fellows of the society and private guests. The trend this year is towards the production of fruit and vegetables in private gardens.

HERE IN BRITAIN

"Champagne Judgement"

Bulmers Cider's claim to a legal right to use the word 'champagne' in the description of their products was overruled in the High Court. Their defence was that 'champagne perry' and 'champagne cider' had been used for generations, therefore the champagne houses could no longer complain.
However, the court was satisfied that people could be misled, believing that Pomagne and Babycham are actually champagne products, and ruled that the champagne houses were entitled to a simple injunction preventing the misuse of the word 'champagne'.

AROUND THE WORLD

"Why Rome Is Without Taxis"

Some 2,750 Rome taxi drivers are on strike until their fares are raised to the level of those in Milan. They also want the prompt payment of state subsidies to taxi licence holders to offset the high price of petrol.

A taxi licence used to be a highly valuable piece of merchandise. To buy one from a driver about to retire, could cost up to 20m lire (about £14,000) and drivers could rent them out or bequeath them to their family. But with falling demand for taxis, the value has dropped to around 16m lire.

Whit Walks

This week, Whit Sunday was celebrated around the world by Catholics, Anglicans and Methodists. This special day is celebrated to commemorate the descent of the Holy Spirit upon Christ's disciples and is the seventh day after Easter or Pentecost, its name deriving from the Anglo-Saxon word 'wit' meaning 'understanding' to celebrate the disciples being filled with the wisdom of the Holy Spirit.

Whit Monday was officially recognised as a bank holiday in 1871 and the day has a special cultural significance in the north-west of England. Many workplaces including factories and cotton mills closed for the whole Whitsuntide week giving workers a holiday and towns held fairs, markets, and parades. Still, a major tradition is the 'Whit Walk' when local churches or chapels employ bands to lead traditional processions through the streets. The origin of these processions dates back to July 1821 when the children of Manchester commemorated the coronation of George IV and children of all denominations walked in procession from their schools and assembled at Ardwick Green to sing 'God Save the King'.

The Bradford Whit Walk has been held continuously since 1903 and is one of the most popular events on the race-walking calendar, attracting hundreds of entries. At the height of its popularity, it attracted top British race walkers and in the 20s and 30s was recognised as the breeding ground for British Olympians, with winners Tommy Green and Harold Whitlock going on to win Olympic gold medals in 1932 and 1936 respectively. This is also the week for many local brass band contests with fierce competition between rival communities and organisations.

May 21st - 27th 1975

IN THE NEWS

Wednesday 21 — **"Commons Win"** An 81 year old resident won her fight to save Bachelors' Acre, New Windsor, as a common for 'sports and pastimes'. The courts confirmed its registration as a town green, and dismissed an appeal by the council, who use it as a car park.

Thursday 22 — **"Medical Loss Causing Concern"** In the past year 284 hospital consultants and 40 senior registrars have emigrated. Most leave for Canada, with others going to America, Australia, New Zealand and Saudi Arabia.

Friday 23 — **"Unemployment Surges Ahead"** The unemployment total rose by 7% to 816,700 this month, which was the biggest monthly rise except for the period of the three-day week last year. At this rate, unemployment could easily reach a million by autumn.

Saturday 24 — **"Prince in The Driving Seat"** Princess Anne was a competitor at The Royal Windsor Horse Show, while Prince Philip put a new carriage through its paces. Both events were closely watched by The Queen and other members of the Royal Family.

Sunday 25 — **"Unexpected Treasure"** Victorian Staffordshire pot lids from cosmetic and food pots proved that a 'find' is still possible. A pot lid bought in Portobello market for £7 fetched £400 at auction after being identified as a very rare example.

Monday 26 — **"Dunkirk Remembered"** An RAF officer dropped a wreath from an RAF helicopter off the French coast in memory of the French and British Servicemen who died on the beaches 35 years ago, and of the 'little ships' destroyed going to their aid.

Tuesday 27 — **"Coach Crash"** A coach crashed through the side of Dibble's Bridge in Yorkshire, dropping 25ft to the river below. The accident happened just outside Hebden Bridge, on the Grassington Road. 32 people were killed and 14 seriously injured.

HERE IN BRITAIN

"Sculpture Display"

An exhibition of more than thirty recent works by 11 of Britain's leading figurative sculptors has been unveiled in Holland Park, London. The exhibition was organised by The Illustrated London News in conjunction with the Greater London Council.
It is the first such exhibition for more than a decade, featuring among others, The iconic 'Boy with a Dolphin' by David Wynne. Opening the exhibition, the deputy leader of the GLC 'chanced his arm' saying, "*As a city, we have got to get back to recognising that art is as important as council housing.*"

AROUND THE WORLD

"Tunnel Invasion Plan Thwarted"

A tunnel stretching 1200 yards from North Korea into South Korea's side of the demilitarised zone has been discovered. The 6ft wide arch-shaped tunnel is tall enough for an average man to stand up in with head room to spare.
The South Koreans estimate that North Korean engineers, in violation of the terms of the armistice treaty, began to construct the tunnel under the southern section of the zone in the middle of 1973. South Koreans patrols in the DMZ reported dull underground explosions in November two years ago.

Cannes Film Festival

Devoted to global competition in the world of film, Cannes, on the Cote D'Azur is the annual focus for all things cinema. Started in 1946, for two weeks each May, this small but perfectly formed town on the French Riviera, is the venue for one of the world's major industries. The official competition with the top award, the Palme d'Or, has not only become a symbol of excellence but a reflection of the changes in the movie industry and continues to inspire new talent.

Previously, in 1938, the International Film Festival was the Mostra in Venice, and that year an American film was the unanimous favourite, but under pressure from Hitler, the Nazi propaganda film 'Olympia' won the Mussolini Cup. Furious, the other countries left Venice determined to hold an alternative festival the following year. A French film festival in Cannes on September 1st, 1939, was advertised. 2,000 invitations were dispatched to all film-producing countries including Germany and Italy, and a transatlantic liner rented by MGM docked in the Bay of Cannes. However, with the announcement of the German-Soviet Pact many tourists fled, and on the 1st of September, Germany invaded Poland and the only film shown that year at a private screening, was 'The Hunchback of Notre-Dame' starring Charles Laughton and Maureen O'Hara. Among other films never screened that year were 'The Wizard of Oz', and Britain's entry 'The Four Feathers'.

This year's festival closed with the film 'Tommy'; a psychedelic musical fantasy film written and directed by Ken Russell and based on the rock group, The Who's, 1969 rock opera album of the same name. There were several bomb scares, and a press conference by Jean-Luc Godard which imparted little real information except that he was preparing a film.

May 28th – June 3rd 1975

IN THE NEWS

Wednesday 28   "**New Grand Master**" The Prince of Wales has been installed as the new Great Master of the Order of the Bath. For many years since its founding in 1399, knights took a ceremonial bath in the Tower of London, hence the name. It is understood Prince Charles, however, did not follow that tradition on this occasion.

Thursday 29   "**The Show Goes On**" Following an accident sustained when jumping over 13 buses on his motorcycle at Wembley Stadium, Evel Knievel, the American stunt man, confirmed his British tour is still on, despite a crushed vertebra, fractured pelvis, a broken hand and bruising.

Friday 30   "**Big Aerospace Deal**" A major deal between British Aerospace and Egypt and Saudi Arabia is nearing completion. This will supply 200 Hawk fighter-trainers, Lynx helicopters, an anti-aircraft missile and two Rolls-Royce jet engines. Egypt will take over the manufacture after 10 years.

Saturday 31   "**European Flights Halted**" A strike by British Airways maintenance crews has caused the cancellation of all the airline's national and European flights out of Heathrow airport.

Sunday June 1   "**Thieves in the Vatican**" The Vatican Court has passed jail sentences on four men, including two former papal gendarmes, for stealing £10,000 worth of stamps and coins from the Vatican administrative offices.

Monday 2   "**Aspro Jobs Lost**" 120 members of the staff at Slough's Aspro-Nicholas research plant are being made redundant following the company's decision to relocate to Paris.

Tuesday 3   "**Radiation Survey**" The National Radiological Protection Board are embarking on a two-year survey into medical radiation. This follows growing concern over the genetic effect of X-rays and possible links to congenital abnormalities.

HERE IN BRITAIN

"Snow Falls on London"

This week saw the first snow and sleet to fall across all parts of the country in summer since 1888. An inch of snow covered the cricket pitch at Buxton in a match between Derbyshire and Lancashire and snowflakes fell briefly on Lord's cricket ground in London.
Arctic winds swept across the UK with temperatures more like winter than early summer. Sleet was reported as far south as Portsmouth, and although it all melted quickly across southern areas of Britain, it lingered on the ground for days in parts of Scotland.

AROUND THE WORLD

"Belting Up"

When Volvo engineer Nils Bohlin invented the 3-point seat belt in 1959 the company decided to make the patent free to all competitors as they prioritised safety over profits.
The Netherlands, along with Norway and Sweden was one of several countries that introduced seat belt legislation this summer, making them mandatory for drivers and front seat passengers. In Holland, before the law, seat belts were used by only 25% of the driving population, but after the law, this increased to 70% across the country.

NATIONAL GARDEN SCHEME

The National Garden Scheme is a charity which raises millions of pounds each year for nursing and health charities, community gardens, and other causes by giving visitors unique access to many exceptional private gardens in the UK. One special garden which opened for just one day in June is Choumert Square. Although it is called 'Square', it is actually a narrow lane-way of 46 tiny cottages and tiny gardens of a secret Southwark street. They have evolved over some 40 years, triggered initially by a few residents' passion for gardening that infused the enthusiasm of others, and they are now a famous London landmark.

The Square was named after the Frenchman, George Choumert who owned the land, and in the 19th Century, had these artisan cottages built. The 1891 Census lists the various occupations of the 106 residents, from bricklayer, dressmaker, and bookbinder, to carpenter, pastry cook and steam engine fitter.

Today the properties are classed as either single occupancy or for a couple, but in the same 1891 census one little house on the North side was home to at least 6 people. Back then, Choumert Square was known to locals as Cut-Throat Lane, so it was obviously far less salubrious than today. Plants seem to thrive in the soil here as it is very rich from past generations when the land was used for market gardening. Today, the Square gardens demonstrate how gardening can unite a community. The street divides into a sunny side and a shady side, which is reflected in the planting. A wide variety of roses provide colour for much of the year against a backdrop of a mixture of trees including birch, willow, and eucalyptus whilst pots are filled with a colourful array of perennial border plants and annuals.

June 4th – 10th 1975

IN THE NEWS

Wednesday 4 — **"Six Monthly Reviews"** The National Federation of Old Age Pensioners are pressing for pensions to be reviewed every six months, payable from the date of agreement, or backdated to the day of the announcement.

Thursday 5 — **"Snowdon Wearing Away"** A report on Snowdon suggests that the mountain is being seriously eroded by the vast number of visitors. It goes on to recommend that the whole area should be managed by a special committee.

Friday 6 — **"Quick Results"** A new method of pregnancy testing, using radioactive isotopes, which gives conclusive results only a week after conception, has been developed by doctors at St Bartholomew's Hospital in London.

Saturday 7 — **"Britain Says Yes"** By a 2:1 majority, the people of Britain have voted 'YES' in the first national referendum to remain in the EEC. Long before all 68 results had been announced, leading opponents of the EEC had conceded victory.

Sunday 8 — **"Just in Time"** Mr Heath, after a busy day, arrived by helicopter just in time to take part in the first trial race to decide the yachts that will represent Britain in the Admiral's Cup. The rules do not permit yachts to start the 220-mile race late.

Monday 9 — **"Parliament on the Radio"** 'Question Time', the initial broadcast from the House of Commons in a radio experiment, had commentators for the BBC and Independent Radio News working in cramped conditions, necessitating precautions so that their remarks were not picked up by the wrong microphone.

Tuesday 10 — **"Search For Substitute May End"** Cigarette manufacturers are to decide whether to abandon the search for a safe cigarette, which has cost more than £10m in the development of the so-called new synthetic smoking materials.

HERE IN BRITAIN

"Home Deliveries"

The Greater London Council is to sponsor an experimental one-year shop-to-home delivery service in an attempt to reduce traffic congestion by shoppers using cars. The scheme will be available to about 500,000 people living in the Lewisham area with the GLC underwriting half the estimated £7,000 direct costs. The service is also aimed to help those people without cars, in particular, the elderly. Customers will have to patronise shops displaying a 'Shoppers' Express' label, and deliveries will be made every weekday morning.

AROUND THE WORLD

"Swiss Vote On Car Ban"

Switzerland is to hold a referendum on whether cars and other private transport should be banned on one Sunday every month, following three trial 'car-less' Sundays during the 1973 oil crisis.

Back then, many people in cities and towns decided that quiet and fresh air justified the inconvenience of using public transport, and will be backing this new initiative. The proposed prohibition of vehicles for 24 hours from 3 am on a Sunday, would apply to cars, motorcycles, private boats and aircraft.

D-DAY ANNIVERSARY

The British film, 'Overlord' was a timely release for the 31st anniversary of the D-Day landings. Archival footage is interwoven with the fictional narrative of a young man's journey from basic training to the front lines on 6th June 1944.

That year, throughout the build-up to D-Day, General Eisenhower used tactics and strategies to mislead the Nazi commanders into thinking the offensive would be staged at the Pas de Calais, rather than the Normandy beaches. Calais was the logical choice for such an attack, being the French point closest to mainland England, thus the deception did not require much convincing. Not only did Eisenhower 'leak' fake information through double agents, including a wild suggestion of Norway being a key landing spot, but also organised practical deceptions. A 'ghost army', under the command of George Patton, was sent to Calais together with a fake Mulberry Harbour, in such a way that it diverted attention away from the Normandy beaches, and many fraudulent radio-transmissions were planted. The day selected for the invasion, the 5th of June, was plagued with exceptionally rough seas, thus it was delayed by a further 24 hours, which increased the risk of German awareness. Nevertheless, the deception element of Operation Overlord proved to be an astounding success, with the Germans being unprepared for an invasion in Normandy.

The film uses archive footage of landing exercises carried out in 1943 and 1944. A giant, 10ft tall, two-wheeled device powered by rockets, called a Panjandrum, had a central hub filled with explosives to be used against obstacles and defences on the landing beaches. However, it never went in a straight line as there was no way to control or steer it after the rockets were fired and was a spectacular failure which was not used in combat.

June 11th – 17th 1975

IN THE NEWS

Wednesday 11 "**Saved from Bankruptcy**" New York City was saved from bankruptcy by a state Bill authorising a Municipal Assistance Corporation, called Big Mac and named after the hamburger, who will take over the debts. The city will have 'to mend its financial ways'.

Thursday 12 "**County Closes School**" Durham County Council have made the first challenge to the NUT advice to teachers not to teach disruptive pupils, by closing a 1,000-pupil school where staff are refusing to teach a 10-year-old boy.

Friday 13 "**IRA Dossiers Missing**" A second set of potentially damaging restricted documents has been found on a rubbish tip near Newry. There is growing controversy over the safety of the army's extensive secret intelligence files on suspected members of the IRA.

Saturday 14 "**Mine Explosion**" The coal board sealed off the faces at Houghton Main colliery in South Yorkshire, where an explosion killed five men last week. The Energy Secretary reminded people of the dangerous price of providing coal.

Sunday 15 "**Holbein Portrait for Sale**" Lord Bradford is negotiating with the British Museum for the sale of the famous Holbein drawing, inscribed with the name of Anne Boleyn. The portrait has been valued at a quarter of a million pounds.

Monday 16 "**British Win at Le Mans**" British team Derek Bell, and Jacky Ickx, won the Le Mans 24-hour motor race in the Gulf Research Racing Team car, finishing nearly two laps ahead of the French team.

Tuesday 17 "**Lord Lucan Accused**" Lady Lucan has identified her husband as her assailant in their home on the night their children's nurse-maid was found battered to death. He tried to strangle her, she said.

HERE IN BRITAIN
"Historic Legislation"

The Magna Carta was signed 760 years ago this week in 1215, and was the first document to put into writing that the king and his government were not above the law. It set out to prevent the king from abusing his power, and placed limits on royal authority by establishing law as a power in itself.

Signed by King John, but only after the rebel barons had forced him to do so, The Magna Carta is considered to be one of the most important legal documents in the English-speaking world and still impacts on legal systems today.

AROUND THE WORLD
"Open-Rear Buses in Paris"

This summer it will be possible to ride on the open rear platform of a Paris bus again, after the practice was abolished amid protests in early 1971.

The new, old-style buses are being re-introduced to please both Parisians and tourists. They will service about 10 routes this summer, but with one difference - the chains which used to let the adventurous leap on and off the rear platform have gone.

Access will now be only through the bus, which, considering the speed and volume of Paris traffic, is probably a wise safety precaution.

Unlucky For Some!

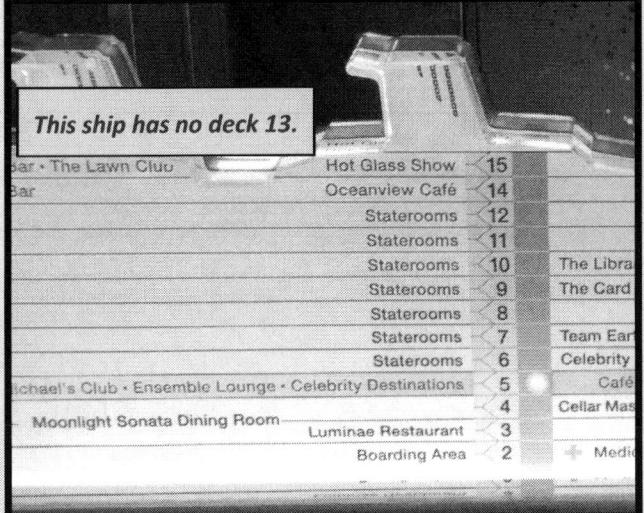

This ship has no deck 13.

When a man woke up and found that his car had been stolen from the drive, then went on the bus to the police station only to trip up as he got off the bus, he might well have wondered about the day and the date. It was Friday 13th. For many, Friday 13th which occurs one to three times per year is regarded as a most unlucky day. Superstitions surrounding the date are thought to originate in the middle-ages and there are dozens of fears, myths and old wives' tales associated with the date all over the world. Some people even suffer from Triskaidekaphobia, the fear or avoidance of the number 13 or 'Paraskevidekatriaphobia', the crippling fear of Friday the 13th.

The number 13 and Friday both have an individual long history of bringing bad luck. In the Bible, Judas, who betrayed Jesus, was the 13th guest to sit down to the Last Supper. In Norse mythology, a dinner party of the gods was ruined by the 13th guest called Loki, 'god of deceit and evil', who caused the world to be plunged into darkness. Peoples of the Mediterranean, regarded 13 with suspicion, not being as perfect as 12, which is divisible in many ways.

As for 'Friday', according to tradition, Adam and Eve were expelled from Eden; Cain murdered Abel; St John the Baptist was beheaded the enactment of the order of Herod for the massacre of the innocents, all took place on a Friday. In Chaucer's Canterbury Tales, written in the 14th Century, he says 'and on a Friday fell all this mischance'. Here in Britain, Friday was once known as 'Hangman's Day' because it was usually when people who had been condemned to death would be hanged and the great crash of 1869, when the price of gold plummeted, was on Friday too.

June 18th - 24th 1975

IN THE NEWS

Wednesday 18 — **"40 Hour Week"** EEC ministers have agreed to introduce a 40-hour working week with four weeks paid holiday a year in Britain. At present, the average annual holiday is three and a half weeks.

Thursday 19 — **"Beagles Stolen"** Two beagles used in experiments with cigarettes, have been stolen by Animal Rights activists, who informed the press *"One of the dogs coughed and wheezed like a human being who has smoked for 30 years"*

Friday 20 — **"Plea for Mercy"** Sir Chandos Blair, has gone to Uganda with an appeal, signed by the Queen, for the life of Mr Dennis Hills, the British lecturer, who is due to be executed, for espionage, by firing squad.

Saturday 21 — **"Struck by Lightning"** A Boeing 747 en route Sydney with 200 people on board was struck by lightning just after leaving Heathrow. The lightning disabled the radar, and hail broke the pilot's window and the landing lights.

Sunday 22 — **"Not A Leg to Stand On"** A 56-year-old London grandmother, was sentenced to two and a half years' imprisonment on smuggling charges. She was arrested in Copenhagen with £4,200 worth of hashish hidden in her artificial leg.

Monday 23 — **"Not a Big Issue"** According to a BBC Advisory Group, violence and sexual explicitness on television can *'sometimes perform a function that is both valuable and valid. Inevitably there are occasional instances of misjudgement, but we are satisfied that those responsible for them are made aware of their failures.'*

Tuesday 24 — **"Save The Whales"** The International Whaling Council met in London to set limits on the hunting of whales. Sir Peter Scott warned whales are on the brink of extinction.

HERE IN BRITAIN
"Tomb Declared Open"

The tomb of Victorian explorer Sir Richard Burton and his wife is listed as a building of historical importance. Burton enthusiasts raised £2,000 to restore the exterior and are now appealing for another £2,000 to restore the exotic interior.

After his death in 1890 Lady Burton built her deceased husband a Bedouin tent in the cemetery of St Mary Magdalen Church, Mortlake. Among its many exotic trappings, was an electrical system which illuminated the interior.

AROUND THE WORLD
"Taking a Tumble"

Singer Alice Cooper took a tumble during the opening number of his concert in Vancouver, when he got tangled up with a toy box prop and ended up 'flipping on his head' into the security barriers.

After going backstage, he learned he'd broken six ribs and suffered a concussion but returned for a few more songs anyway - and later pledged to continue the tour saying his fall was *'such a silly thing'*. *'I cracked my ribs and hit my head on the cement floor. But we came back on in that old 'show-must-go-on' bit.'*

WIMBLEDON CHAMPIONSHIP

Billie Jean King won the 1975 Ladies Singles. Arthur Ashe won the Men's Singles

This week at Wimbledon, Billie Jean King of America defeated Australia's Evonne Goolagong Cawley 6-0, 6-1 to win her 6th Wimbledon Ladies Singles title and Arthur Ashe of the USA beat Jimmy Connors, also of America, 6-1, 6-1, 5-7, 6-4, to win his first Wimbledon title.

The first Championships were organised by the All England Croquet and Lawn Tennis Club in 1877 and was for men only. Twenty-two players entered, providing their own racquets and shoes whilst the club's gardener provided the tennis balls with their hand-sewn flannel outer casings. As lawn tennis was a popular sport, interest in the championships grew, and by 1884, when women were finally allowed to compete, regularly drew crowds numbering 3,000. By 1900, doubles and mixed doubles matches were also a regular part of the programme, as were players from overseas, but Britain dominated the winners until 1905 when an American claimed the Women's Singles title.

Although not classed as a regular Olympic sport, it did feature in 1908 when London hosted the games and the first televised Wimbledon broadcast was made in June 1937 with the programme limited to 30 minutes. During the first world war, the championships were held as usual, but many players didn't compete either because they took active roles in combat or were prisoners of war. Two German players, being members of Kaiser Wilhelm's personal staff, were held in British prison camps for the duration of the war. However, during WW2, for six years from 1940, no tennis was played at Wimbledon. In October 1940 a bomb hit the Centre Court causing extensive damage to the stands, meaning when the Championship re-opened in 1946, fewer spectators could be accommodated. Wimbledon is the most sought-after title in tennis because it's "the granddaddy of them all."

June 25th – July 1st 1975

IN THE NEWS

Wednesday 25 — **"The Elusive Lord"** The search for Lord Lucan, wanted for the murder of Mrs Sandra Rivett, the nursemaid to his three children, is being concentrated along the coastal border area between France and Belgium.

Thursday 26 — **"County Hospital – A Medical Slum"** The 24 leading doctors at the Royal Hampshire County Hospital in Winchester complain in an open letter of "*the medically dangerous conditions of a 19th century building*", describing it as a medical slum.

Friday 27 — **"Royal Visit"** The Queen made a tour of the new Covent Garden fruit and vegetable market at Vauxhall in London, after unveiling a plaque to commemorate the occasion during the official opening ceremony.

Saturday 28 — **"Aston Martin Saved"** Aston Martin has been bought for just over £1m by an Anglo-American-Canadian consortium including a young British entrepreneur who is remaining anonymous. This puts the company officially on the road to recovery.

Sunday 29 — **"Struck by Lightning"** The golfers Lee Trevino and Jerry Heard were struck by lightning during a thunderstorm while playing in the Western Open golf tournament in Chicago. Trevino said, "*My whole life flashed before me.*"

Monday 30 — **"Crocodile Licences"** A proposal is before parliament that live crocodiles, alligators, and all species of turtles can only be imported into Britain under licence. There is widespread acceptance now that all species of crocodylia need conservation.

Tuesday 1 July — **"Childhood Diabetes"** Childhood diabetes may be three or four times more common in Britain than previously believed. The latest figures show that there are 25,000 children under 16 with diabetes, compared with a previously quoted figure of 7,000.

HERE IN BRITAIN
"New, Cheaper Escort!"

In response to the depressed car market, Ford has rushed out the new, low-priced Escort Popular. The new version of the iconic Escort starts at £1,299, which is £141 less than the previous cheapest model. The Popular, was planned only three months ago by Ford's managing director when he decided the company needed a cheaper car to compete against foreign imports. Retailing at £70 less than the best-selling foreign car, the Japanese Datsun Sunny, £106 less than the Renault 5 and £35 less than the Mini 1000, it also claims up to 15 % better fuel economy.

AROUND THE WORLD
"The Cost of Dying"

The West Germans though successful in restraining the cost of living, are less so in keeping down the cost of dying. The average cost of an interment is £518, double the cost five years ago. Municipal burial charges have risen by 800% and the price of a death certificate has trebled. Even the cost of tolling a bell has risen from 72p to £3.50. Despite the enormous rise in costs, the demand for a suitable, middle-class funeral remains steady. This means big business for the undertakers, as 725,000 people died in West Germany last year.

ROYAL HIGHLAND SHOW

The Royal Highland Show at Edinburgh is an annual event that showcases Scotland's farming, food, and rural life. The first show was in 1822, and each year, it travelled around the country. However, building new sites each year became increasingly difficult and costly, stand holders complained of soaring prices, and arguments for hosting the Show at a permanent site grew louder, until the organisers agreed that a permanent home was needed, making it easier for visitors, competitors and exhibitors alike, and providing a national exhibition site that would put Scotland firmly on the map.

Aside from the livestock events, the show features competitions, including the Scottish Handcrafts Championships, the Scottish Honey Championships, and the Technical Innovation and Scottish Dairy Produce Championships. But unique to this occasion are displays of highland dancing, and pipe bands featuring the famous musical instrument of Scotland – the bagpipes.

The great Highland bagpipe has been around since the 15th century and has since achieved the widespread importance it enjoys today, whereas other bagpipe traditions throughout Europe, from Portugal to Russia, almost all went into decline by the early 20th century. Although their prominence declined when the Jacobite Rebellion was quashed in 1746, they still formed part of the musical tradition of warfare to stir up the hearts of fighting men and were last used in the battle of El Alamein in 1943. The Highland bagpipe plays a role as both a solo and ensemble instrument. En masse, it forms part of a complete pipe band accompanied only by drums, but the most recognised instance of it as a solo instrument is the position of Piper to the Sovereign, which dates back to the time of Queen Victoria, who always had a piper play on the terrace of Balmoral, while the family were at breakfast.

July 2nd – 8th 1975

IN THE NEWS

Wednesday 2   **"Below the Mark"** It has been announced that 60% of the doctors from overseas who took the General Medical Council's first compulsory language and medical competence tests last week, have failed.

Thursday 3   **"Magna Carta On Loan"** For the bicentennial celebrations of American independence, this year, the British Library reference division is to lend to the United States Congress one of its four original copies of the Magna Carta.

Friday 4   **"Men's Life Expectancy Static"** The rising number of coronary thromboses means that the average life expectancy of men is not improving. The main causes of thromboses are lack of physical activity, a poor diet high in fat, and cigarette smoking.

Saturday 5   **"NIMBYism"** The Inner London area urgently needs plants for the treatment and disposal of toxic waste, but while the residents fully appreciate this, they vehemently oppose all plans to build them anywhere near where they live.

Sunday 6   **"Move Towards Women's Ordination"** The Church of England General Synod has taken a cautious step towards the ordination of women priests, by declaring that it has no fundamental objections to the plan.

Monday 7   **"Visitors Pose Threat to Water Supply"** It is feared that the influx of summer visitors to the Southwest will seriously impact water supplies. The Bude area currently has only 15 day's supply left and standpipes are being made ready.

Tuesday 8   **"Doctors Back Free Contraceptives"** Doctors at the annual conference of the British Medical Association defeated a motion condemning the free provision of contraceptives, in spite of a popular view, that *"it was a frivolous use of money in a service to the healthy while the seriously ill had to pay prescription charges"*.

HERE IN BRITAIN

"80 Years Old"

The National Trust held a royal garden party to celebrate its 80th anniversary. Founded in 1895, it has become the greatest conservation society and largest private landowner in Britain. The venue was Montacute House in Somerset, built in the reign of Elizabeth I.

More than 2,000 members and benefactors of the Trust attended, some of whom had come for tea from as far away as North America and South Africa. Queen Elizabeth the Queen Mother arrived by helicopter from Buckingham Palace and was taken on a tour of the house.

AROUND THE WORLD

"Noonday Gun Continues"

The historic noonday gun on Hong Kong's waterfront has defeated a charge of noise pollution brought by a mother in a neighbouring apartment, who claimed that the noise frightened her child. The complaint caused much indignation in the Hong Kong Club and among older residents, who respect the gun as one of the colony's ancient traditions. Noel Coward's famous song immortalised this in the words, *"In Hong Kong they strike a gong and fire off a midday gun, but mad dogs and Englishmen go out in the noon day sun."*

72 Peaks In A Day

This year, the title, 'The Greatest of Them All', has been bestowed on Joss Naylor, when he ran 72 Lake District mountains, claimed to involve over 100 miles and about 38,000 feet of ascent, in 23 hours and 11 minutes.

A Lake District sheep farmer in the isolated valley of Wasdale and fell runner, Naylor has set many long-distance records. He was born in 1936 and left school at 15 to work on the family farm where early injuries caused him to undergo several operations, including spinal surgery in 1958 to remove two discs from his back. As part of his rehabilitation, he took up running, winning his first race, the Mountain Trial, in 1966. Five years later he completed the 'Bob Graham Round' only the sixth person to do so since the record was set in 1932 by Bob Graham, a Keswick guest-house owner. The challenge to traverse 42 fells within a 24-hour period, starting and finishing at Keswick Moot Hall, involves a distance of 66 miles with 26,900' of ascent.

Naylor's greatest record, however, is still unbroken - The National Three Peaks Challenge, which he smashed in 1971. This covers a total walking distance of 23 miles with an ascent of 10,052 feet, to the summits of Britain's highest mountains of Scafell Pike in England, Ben Nevis in Scotland and Snowdon in Wales within 24 hours, including driving time. Incredibly he managed to complete this with plenty of time to spare in under 12 hours. Helped by lorry driver Frank Davies, who drove the 462 miles between the peaks in a rally-specification Ford Capri, Naylor set a record in driving rain that will probably never be beaten. *"It was just one of those magic things."*

July 9th – 15th 1975

IN THE NEWS

Wednesday 9 — "Leaving School Early" An Act was debated in parliament proposes to allow all pupils who have reached the age of 16 to leave school at the spring Bank holiday instead of waiting until the end of the summer term.

Thursday 10 — "Brighton's West Pier Closing" Brighton's 109-year-old West Pier, regarded as the finest example of a Victorian pleasure pier in Britain, is to close because it has become unsafe.

Friday 11 — "Number Plates to Go" Motor cyclists will no longer have to carry front number plates, as the sharp metal edges are too dangerous for riders and pedestrians. However rear number plates will remain compulsory.

Saturday 12 — "Cutting Their Losses" In an attempt to reduce costs, The Financial Times, regarded as one of the safest newspapers financially, are moving to computerised production and shedding 35% of their staff.

Sunday 13 — "No Jobs Here" Job prospects for school leavers in Wales this summer are the worst for 30 years, and up to 10,000 young people are likely to be left unemployed. The Welsh TUC said, *"The social consequences, an increase in vandalism, other crime, frustration and migration, will be appalling."*

Monday 14 — "Workers Denial" Workers at a Sunderland furniture factory have been accused of laziness and vandalism. Wash basins have been smashed and lavatory seats ripped out and as a result the factory has failed to meet delivery dates, and is having to shut down"

Tuesday 15 — "Roadside Savings" In order to save up to £1m, the Department of the Environment is to stop cutting grass on motorways and trunk roads, except in special cases where the vegetation impedes visibility.

HERE IN BRITAIN

"St. Brendan"

A crew from Dublin aim to show that the Irish discovered America first. A curragh named 'The Brendan' will be shaped like a 36ft long banana and built to the traditional Celtic form. The wickerwork frame, covered with 25 ox hides greased with cod oil and tallow, will also be dressed with butter during the voyage.

With oars and two square sails made of leather, the crew comprising a meteorologist, a cameraman, a sailing master, and a navigator from the Irish Naval Service will have modern navigational equipment too to guide them.

AROUND THE WORLD

"Snake-tease"

Ten years ago Glenda Kemp began stripping with "Oupa" her pet python in Johannesburg. Her scandalous actions and her provocative moves caused the South African Vice Squad to do their best to stop her, without success.

Faced with barricades of Christian wives on one side and loyal fans and liberals on the other, she never gave up but continued to provoke the attention of the public. However, the striptease dancer, has now been fined £200 and given a suspended six-month jail sentence, for dancing naked with a python at a private gathering of pigeon fanciers.

St Swithun's Day

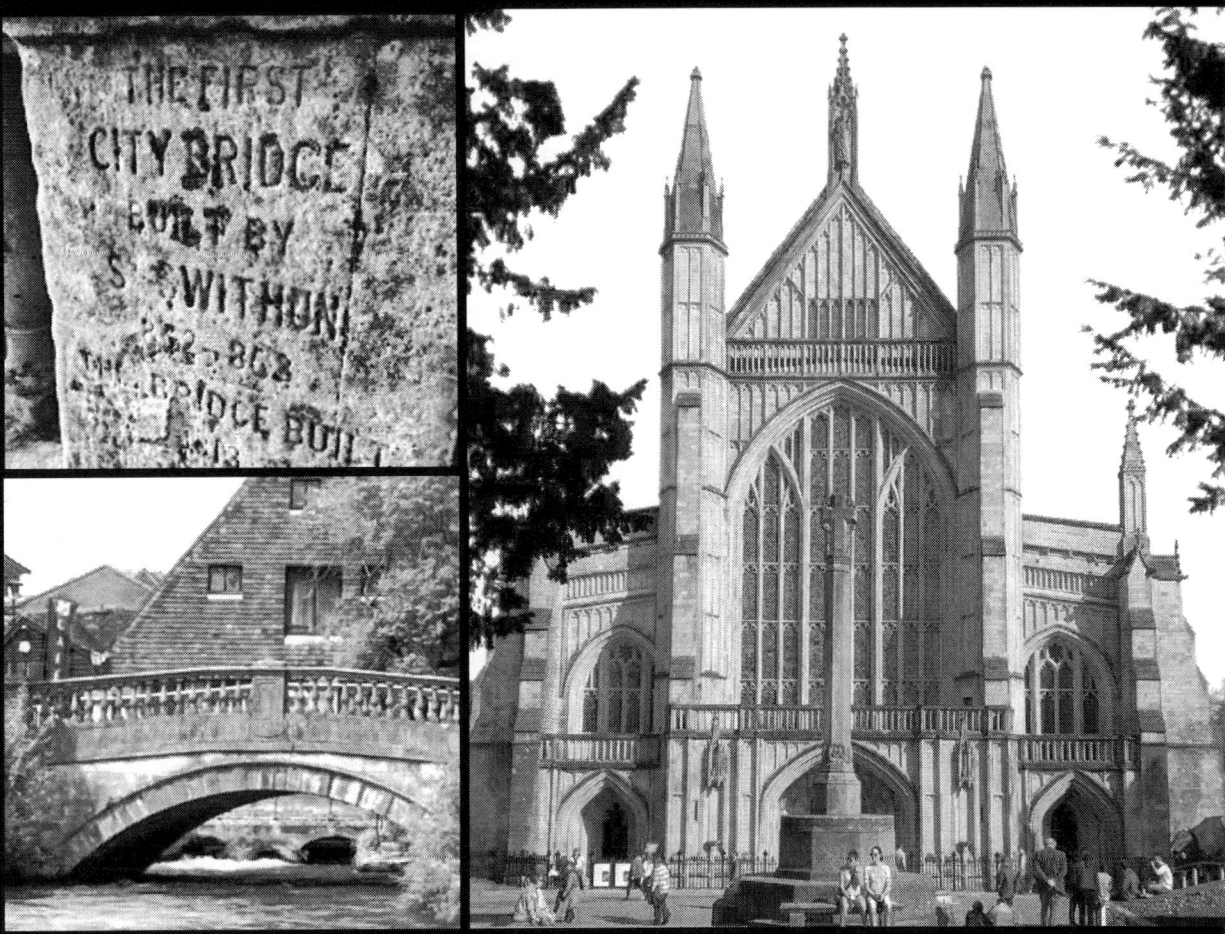

St. Swithun was an Anglo-Saxon bishop of Winchester in the 9th century. Noted for humility, he was popular with the people. On his deathbed Swithin begged to be buried outside the north wall of his cathedral, unlike other religious nobility who were buried close to the altar. He wanted to be where passers-by walked, and rain fell on it. In 971 AD, the restoration and enlargement of the building was completed, and Swithin was adopted as the cathedral's patron saint. To mark the occasion, Swithun's body was dug up and re-interred on 15th July, with much ceremony, in the new cathedral behind the altar.

Numerous miracles were reported following the move. The two most famous 'miracles' are those of the Winchester egg-seller, and Queen Emma's ordeal. A woman was going to sell a basket of eggs at market. They were snatched by some workmen as a prank and got broken. In tears she prayed to St Swithun, and the eggs were 'miraculously' restored. Queen Emma, the mother of Edward the Confessor, was accused of having an affair, and to prove her innocence had to walk on red hot ploughshares. The night before her ordeal she prayed to St Swithun, and the next day was able to walk on the hot metal without injury.

According to tradition, if it rains on Saint Swithun's bridge, opposite Winchester Water Mill, on 15th July, it will rain for forty days. There is a scientific basis for this, which is that around mid-July, the jet stream settles into a pattern which holds reasonably steady until the end of August. When it lies north of Britain, continental high pressure moves in; but when it lies across or south of Britain, cooler and wetter Atlantic weather systems predominate.

July 16th - 22nd 1975

IN THE NEWS

Wednesday 16 — **"Iceland Extends Limit"** The Icelandic Government has announced a unilateral extension to the fishing limit from 50 miles to 200 miles which will impact severely on the price and availability of fresh fish in Great Britain.

Thursday 17 — **"Most Expensive Watercolour"** Turner's famous watercolour, "The Dark Rigi", has been sold to an undisclosed buyer at Sotheby's for £85,000, making it the most expensive English watercolour ever sold at auction.

Friday 18 — **"Court Will Sit Late"** The court at Bow Street, London, will be kept open until late for the arrival from Australia of the runaway MP John Stonehouse, and secretary Sheila Buckley, to face charges of fraud, theft and conspiracy.

Saturday 19 — **"Tunnel Vision"** Railway enthusiasts are excavating a lost tunnel at Crystal Palace and hope to discover what might have been the earliest underground passenger train in Britain. The train, blown along by compressed air and designed by a Victorian engineer, ran between 1864 and 1865.

Sunday 20 — **"Butter Production Stopped"** An increasing shortage of milk due to poor grass growth, and increased slaughter of dairy cattle, has led the Milk Marketing Board to call for a halt to production of butter for the foreseeable future.

Monday 21 — **"Reservoir Polluted"** Ten thousand people in Rochdale and six Lancashire villages are without a mains water supply, after traces of phenol, a chemical used in the plastics industry, was discovered in the nearby Cowm Reservoir.

Tuesday 22 — **"Parking Fines Increase"** The Home Office has announced that fixed penalties for parking offences will increase from £2 to £6. The registered owner of the car will be liable for parking even if they were not driving at the time.

HERE IN BRITAIN

"Chawton Festival"

Like many English villages, Chawton in Hampshire, celebrated summer with a fete, the likes of which could well have been enjoyed by the village's most celebrated inhabitant, Jane Austen, who was born 200 years ago.

Schoolchildren danced round the maypole and the church where Jane's mother and sister are buried, was decorated with flowers. Pilgrims inspected Jane's house and furniture, the oak she planted and the views she described, walking the paths she trod.

AROUND THE WORLD

"Trek Across the Alps"

19 men and one woman from the Transport Corps set off on a 15-day training exercise, marching 170 miles across the French Alps following the route used by Hannibal's army in 218 BC. They marched from Die, in the Alpes du Dauphine, to the Col de la Traversette on the Italian frontier.

They tried riding on an elephant to experience what it would have been like in Hannibal's day, but the elephant was only on temporary loan from a safari park, so most of the party will have to walk, as did Hannibal's troops.

Ladies of 'La Nuit'

Today there are some 30,000 prostitutes in France, half of them in the Paris region, suffering from increasing police harassment and many have now gone on strike, demanding official recognition, the ability to lead a normal life outside of work, and to be able to keep their children. *"We are ready to pay reasonable taxes, national health, and even to contribute to a pension fund – why not?"* The protest which started in Lyons has spread rapidly, and prostitutes in many major cities are staging sit-ins in large churches and cathedrals as 'sanctuaries of freedom', including the Chapel of St Bernard, in the Montparnasse area, where about 200 women were visited by writer and feminist Mme Simone de Beauvoir, who suggested that they submit their demands to Mme Veil, the Minister of Health.

Prostitution in France, similar to that in other European countries, experienced alternating periods of tolerance and repression, often being integrated into society rather than being marginalised. The great Cathedral of Chartres had a window depicting the parable of The Prodigal Son which was endowed by prostitutes in the same way as other windows were endowed by various other trade guilds or private benefactors.

The brightly coloured house numbers of Parisian houses were often a clue as to what lay beyond the gates – The One-Two-Two was one of the most luxurious and illustrious brothels of Paris in the 1930s and 1940s. The name was taken from the address, 122 Rue de Provence, with a gaudy gold and blue number decoration sitting above the thick wrought iron gates to help guide the curious towards it. The numbers were translated into English to ensure that foreign tourists would be able to find the brothel and as a password for French people.

July 23rd - 29th 1975

IN THE NEWS

Wednesday 23 — **"Harsh Words"** Prince Phillip apologised for calling the members of the Agricultural Development Service the parasites of agriculture. *"Some people believe that my comments were too lively. I must admit they looked a good deal rougher in cold print than they sounded at the time."*

Thursday 24 — **"Rooftop Protest"** A prisoner who escaped from Kirkham prison in Lancashire, resisted re-arrest with his five-year-old son, for nine hours. He was refused parole despite good behaviour and made his rooftop protest 'against the disheartening parole system'.

Friday 25 — **"Road Maintenance Cuts"** Spending on trunk road maintenance will be cut by 20% over the next three years, by using surface dressings rather than complete resurfacing, less footpath repairs and less grass cutting.

Saturday 26 — **"BBC Quits India"** The BBC stated the new Indian censorship regulations prevent giving 'a fair and authentic picture of events in India' and suspended its news operations in India. Mark Tully, the correspondent, will leave immediately for London.

Sunday 27 — **"Cruel Practice"** The use of cinch-straps round the hind quarters of horses in an American-style rodeo in Sussex was condemned as cruel. The rodeo organisers denied that the straps were used to *inflict pain* in order to make the horses 'buck'.

Monday 28 — **"Shoddy Shoes"** The footwear Industry, which is troubled by foreign imports and sluggish home orders, has been criticised by the Office of Fair Trading, for 'a pretty dismal record' for customer service, with many complaints about shoddy goods.

Tuesday 29 — **"Colour TV For London Schools"** As an alternative to the BBC and ITV Schools programmes, Inner London Schools are to get their own colour television service using the Education Authority's closed-circuit television system.

HERE IN BRITAIN

"Tarting Up"

The Northwest Thames Regional Health Authority has discovered a surplus of £106,726 in their finances as the London Ambulance Service's proposed expenditure for this year turned out to be lower than had been allowed for.

They are therefore considering spending £28,175 of it on furniture, equipment and redecoration of its headquarters. The proposal, which at a time when the National Health Service is failing for lack of money, has caused quite a controversy.

AROUND THE WORLD

"Fortunes Combined"

Christina Onassis, daughter of the shipping magnate Aristotle Onassis, married the son of banker and shipowner, Alexander Andreades, uniting two of Greece's great fortunes.

The marriage surprised Greek society as the bride was thought to be considering becoming engaged to Petros Goulandris, a member of another Greek shipping family. The bride, who inherited the bulk of her father's $1,000m (about £453m) estate, had promised him on his death bed last March to marry Goulandris, but the romance did not develop.

WORLDLY ESPERANTO

The 60th annual congress of the World Esperanto Federation, the Universala Kongresso, was held in Copenhagen, attended by around 1200 delegates from some sixty countries and introduced by the President of the federation, a British-born Professor of English Literature who teaches in Philadelphia. Although Esperanto is not a major world language, it has quite a following today, particularly in Europe and parts of the Far East, and it began as the idea of a Polish doctor in the 1880's, who believed having a common language could bring the global community closer together.

Although Dr Zamenhof's dream of world peace never materialised, the language lives on. Based on European languages, it is easy to learn and pronounce. Although a medical doctor, Zamenhof was no amateur at languages, speaking nine fluently and having a working knowledge of three of the classical languages, Latin, Hebrew and Aramaic, from school days! Many devotees abandoned Esperanto with the onset of World War I, seeing the ideal of world peace disintegrating, and later in World War II, it was banned by Hitler, who wrote in Mein Kampf that it was *'a language being used by Jews as a method of world domination.'* However, with the end of the war there was a slow resurgence of interest, as travel and trade were opened up again, and international agencies such as NATO and UNESCO were formed and the United Nations became more prominent on the world stage.

Not only is the language used in international business circles, but many books and plays have been translated into Esperanto. Among famous people who speak it fluently are the author J.R.R.Tolkien, Harold Wilson the PM, and William Shatner, from the television series 'Star Trek', who learnt it specially for his part in the film 'Incubus'.

July 30th - Aug 5th 1975

IN THE NEWS

Wednesday 30 — **"Skytrain Cancelled"** Freddie Laker, chairman of Laker Airways, has reacted strongly to a decision by the Government to cancel his cheap Skytrain Transatlantic Service, saying, '*I am going to fight it in the courts if necessary.*'

Thursday 31 — **"Cottage Industry in Jail"** An inmate of Maidstone Jail aided by two fellow prisoners, set up to the bespoke manufacture of cheque books and cheque cards. The three prisoners have all admitted conspiracy to defraud at Canterbury Crown Court

Friday 1 Aug — **"Rising Health Costs"** The DHSS has stated in its annual report that the cost of prescriptions issued by doctors rose by £40m last year, with 10 million more being issued.

Saturday 2 — **"Stealing Own Van"** A father and son, both market traders in Erith, Kent, have been accused of stealing their own van from a Gloucester garage after refusing to pay £95 for the repair work carried out. The pair maintained it was still under warranty.

Sunday 3 — **"Reluctant Parenting"** The Office of Population Censuses and Surveys has confirmed that the trend for couples to put off having children due to the uncertain and volatile current economic situation, is likely to continue.

Monday 4 — **"Royal Birthday"** Queen Elizabeth the Queen Mother celebrated her seventy-fifth birthday. A royal gun salute was fired in her honour by The King's Troop of The Royal Horse Artillery in Hyde Park at noon.

Tuesday 5 — **"Temperatures Soar"** Temperatures reached 34C (93F) in parts of Gloucestershire and Hampshire, and up to 32C (90F) in Blackpool and parts of East Anglia.

HERE IN BRITAIN

"A Corrosive Menace"

A report on 'Dogs in the UK' has been heavily criticised for underplaying the problem of dogs fouling in public places. It fails to mention the dogs' success in causing the collapse of lamp standards by urinating against them.

Up to 3,000 pints of corrosive canine urine are released in London each day, causing standards to be taken down because they had become unstable and dangerous. A foreman of a maintenance team said, *"Look on the columns about 2' up from the ground, you will see a band where the dogs have obviously fouled frequently."*

AROUND THE WORLD

"Sacred Cows for Auction"

Hindus see the cow as a sacred animal and as a source of prosperity. Untended sacred cows in Delhi, which up until now have been allowed to wander freely about the city, will in future be rounded up and auctioned off by the city authorities.

Previously the animals, which caused serious traffic jams and occasionally accidents, as well as chewing their cud in the shade of trees in public parks and depositing their dung where people need to walk, were picked up and later returned to their owners after a small fine had been paid. These same owners will now have to be more responsible with their animals.

Paternoster

A bronze sculpture by Elizabeth Frink, 'Paternoster' has been unveiled in Paternoster Square, in the City of London, by the famous violinist Mr Yehudi Menuhin. The statue is of an androgynous shepherd herding five sheep and reflects the former use of Paternoster Row as the site of Newgate Market where livestock and meat were traded. Being in the shadow of St. Paul's Cathedral in the City of London, some say it also represents the Good Shepherd and may also play on the linguistic similarity between the Latin words for The Lords Prayer - Paternoster and for shepherd - pastor.

Historically this area included St Paul's Cross and Paternoster Row and became one of the principal marketplaces in London. St Paul's Cross was an open-air pulpit from which many of the most important statements on the political and religious changes brought about during the Reformation were made public during the sixteenth and seventeenth centuries. Only one execution is recorded as taking place in St Paul's Churchyard, being that of Henry Garnet, for his part in the Gunpowder plot.

The street is supposed to have received its name from the fact that it was the main place in London where paternoster or rosary beads were made. The beads were popular with faithful Catholics who prayed their beads every day. From the 17th century Paternoster Row was a centre of the London publishing trade but the street was devastated by aerial bombardment during the Blitz of World War II. It suffered particularly heavy damage in the night raid of 29–30 December 1940, which has been called the 'Second Great Fire of London' during which an estimated five million books were lost in the fires caused by tens of thousands of incendiary bombs.

Aug 6th - 12th 1975

IN THE NEWS

Wednesday 6 — **"Thames Escape"** Four businessmen and their pilot were winched from the water, when their helicopter engine failed just after they had taken off from a barge at King's Reach, and they plummeted from about 20ft into the Thames near Blackfriars Bridge.

Thursday 7 — **"Arsenic Levels"** The Ministry of Agriculture has ordered an examination of the amount of arsenic allowed in food. It is now an offence to sell food containing more than one part in a million of arsenic.

Friday 8 — **"Pledge to End Tied Cottages"** The Government is to abolish tied cottages on farms and give 70,000 farm workers the protection of the Rent Acts against eviction.

Saturday 9 — **"Social Workers Strike"** More than 200 social workers in the London borough of Tower Hamlets went on strike for a day to protest against under staffing in their department, and Union officials warned of further strikes if cuts to public spending continue.

Sunday 10 — **"Football Rowdies"** One of Britain's leading judges has said that if he could *'turn the clock back, he would happily put football hooligans in the stocks on Saturday afternoons. Decent supporters could then look on them with the utter contempt they deserved.'*

Monday 11 — **"Not Amused"** Mary Whitehouse of the National Viewers and Listeners' Association, criticised Betty Ford, wife of the US President, for saying, *'that in general premarital relations 'with the right partner' might reduce the divorce rate,'* by accusing her of *'encouraging promiscuity and approving of premarital sex.'*

Tuesday 12 — **"Miners' Blood Check"** Researchers are asking 2,000 miners to give blood samples, as part of a drive to establish the causes of pneumoconiosis, a major cause of death among pit workers.

HERE IN BRITAIN

"Rutland Water"

Work has begun demolishing the houses and farms of Nether Hambleton, an English village in the idyllic and rural part of Rutland, which has been selected as the site of a new reservoir to serve the rapidly expanding population of Southeast England. New homes are desperately needed, but so too is their increasing demand for fresh water, and this was chosen as the perfect location for 'Rutland Water'. A protective bank of earth and stones is currently being banked up around Normanton Church, part of which will be above the surface of the reservoir.

AROUND THE WORLD

"Dams Collapse"

Typhoon Nina has devastated parts of the Henan area of Eastern China, catastrophically causing 62 dams including the Bangiao Dam to collapse, killing 229,000 people, and destroying 6 million homes. More than the normal yearly rainfall fell in one day creating the third most deadly flood in history, covering three million acres of agricultural land and 30 cities, wiping out infrastructure, communications, livestock and crops. The dams that collapsed were constructed during the 'Great Leap Forward' with the help of Soviet advisers.

New Cruise Ships

With the advent of large passenger jet aircraft in the 1960s, intercontinental travellers switched from ships to planes, sending the ocean liner trade into a steady decline. This year a revival in the popularity of cruising has been forecast, as construction has begun on a new fleet of Scandinavian-designed ships, which will be part of the Princess Cruises' growing fleet, so named because they will be the follow-on generation of floating palaces from the 'Queens' which brought such glamour to ocean travel. Cruising is now marketed as an all inclusive holiday, rather than a way of getting from A to B.

Cruise holidays have been around since P&O first introduced passenger-cruising services in **1844** to destinations such as Gibraltar, Malta and Athens, sailing from Southampton. Notable ships of the era include SS *Valetta* built in 1889, which was the first ship to use electric lights. The Hamburg-America Line was the first to send their transatlantic ships out on long southern cruises during the worst of the North Atlantic winter seasons, and the idea of a 'Winter Cruise' was born - an ideal break from the chilly Northern winter months.

During the 19th Century larger and more luxurious ships were commissioned Titanic being the most famous example, offering fine dining, luxury services and staterooms with finer appointments. Cruising in these times even gave us the word 'posh'. On long journeys, particularly those between the UK and India, wealthier passengers would demand cabins that were shadier in the afternoon so they would be cooler by bedtime, which would be the port side going out and the starboard side coming back, or Port Out Starboard Home, which was stamped on the ticket.

Aug 13th - 19th 1975

IN THE NEWS

Wednesday 13   "Early Closing" Managers of 600 public houses in the Midlands have reached the decision to close their pubs indefinitely in an attempt to force brewery draymen to join the Transport and General Workers' Union.

Thursday 14   "Alumina Cement Safe" The Government report investigating the collapse of a school building in Stepney at the beginning of this year, has announced that most homes containing high-alumina cement are structurally safe.

Friday 15   "High Price of Violence" The cost of policing outside football grounds because of fan violence, cost the public in England and Wales £750,000 last year.

Saturday 16   "Cosmic Ray Mystery" The world's most accurate radio telescope at Cambridge is leading an urgent worldwide search to pinpoint the source of the most dramatic event seen by modern astronomers. An increasingly intense concentration of X-rays in outer space, which surpasses Crab Nebula, currently the brightest known object.

Sunday 17   "Epic Cloudburst" A cloudburst in London, after weeks of sub-tropical weather, provided unprecedented data for meteorologists, when 2-3 million tons of rain fell on a 6sq mile area of North London, causing floods and disrupting transport.

Monday 18   "PM In Burglary" A book due to be published claims that within the past 10 years a British Prime Minister arranged for a detective to 'burgle' a senior politician's flat. The author said they were satisfied with the evidence they have.

Tuesday 19   "School Leavers Lack Basics" Many school-leavers are starting their first jobs without having mastered even the basic essentials of reading, writing and arithmetic.

HERE IN BRITAIN

"Outlook Changeable"

New BBC TV weather symbols are to be introduced to give viewers a clearer understanding after complaints that triangles (representing showers) and dots (rain) are not sufficiently intelligible. The new system uses symbols, utilising one 'cloud', black for those threatening rain and white for others.

From it will emerge blue teardrops (rain), yellow flashes (lightning) or yellow rays to illustrate that every cloud has a silver lining. Fog, however, will not have a symbol, it remains as FOG. Satellite pictures of the weather will also be shown regularly on television.

AROUND THE WORLD

"Svalbard Airport"

Svalbard, over 500 miles north of Norway is the most northerly airport in the world with scheduled public flights. Construction started in 1973, and the airport has just been officially opened by King Olav V.

The first airstrip on Svalbard was constructed by the Luftwaffe during WWII, but due to the lack of runway lights, flights were only permitted during summer, the sun never rising in winter. The airport is built on permafrost, so the runway is insulated against the ground to prevent it melting the underlying ground during the summer.

WILLIAM WALLACE

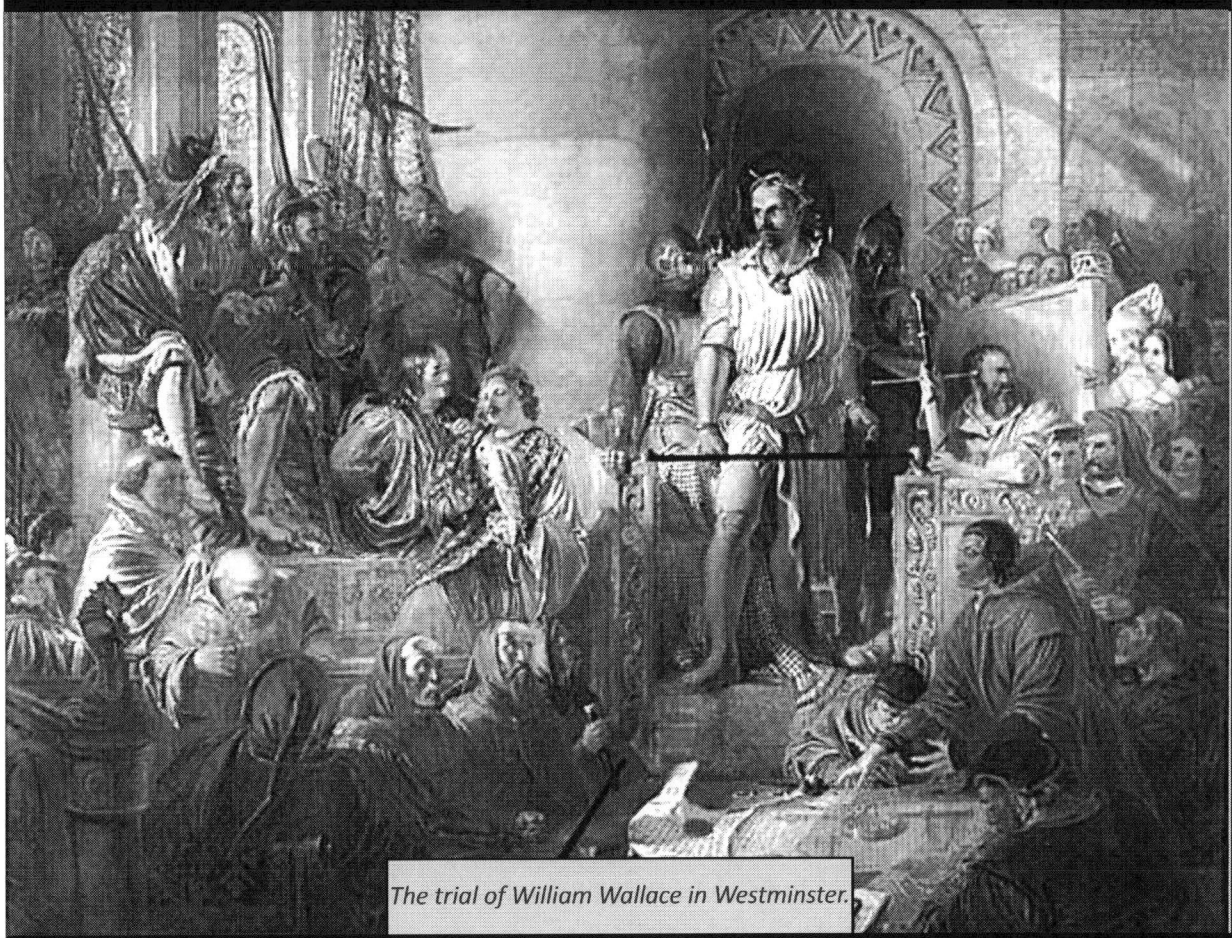
The trial of William Wallace in Westminster.

August 23rd is the 670th anniversary this month of the execution of the Scottish patriot, and national hero, Sir William Wallace, at Smithfield, London, the Wallace Memorial Committee announced details of a memorial tablet to be set in a panel in the wall of St. Bartholomew's Hospital, near the spot where he was executed. The slab is of Creetown granite and will be set in the wall panel, surrounded by a metal railing. The slab will have an inscription, cut and leaded, and bronze and enamel ornaments in appropriate colours. The crown at the top is a replica of the Scottish crown at the time of Wallace and the lower lion, mounted between blue and white saltire crosses, is Wallace's coat of arms.

Wallace, a Scottish knight, roused the spirit of Scotland and became one of the leaders during the First War of Scottish Independence which followed the invasion of Scotland by England in 1296. Most famously, he led the rebellion against Edward I, inflicting the defeat of the English army at Stirling Bridge. Wallace then became the Guardian of Scotland and served until his defeat at the Battle of Falkirk in July 1298.

In August 1305, Wallace was betrayed and captured near Glasgow and brought, in chains, to London, where he was tried, found guilty of treason and sentenced to death. Using one of the most brutal executions of the medieval era, on 23rd August, he was hung, drawn and quartered at the Bartholomew's Fair, Smithfield, following which, to act as a deterrent to other would be rebels, his head was dipped in tar and placed on a pike on London Bridge whilst his arms and legs were sent to be displayed in Newcastle, Berwick, Stirling and Perth.

AUG 20TH - 26TH 1975

IN THE NEWS

Wednesday 20 — *"ASH Ban"* Action on Smoking and Health want to ban the royal warrant being used in cigarette advertisements on the grounds that it infringes the advertising code that '… *should not claim, directly or indirectly, the recommendation of a particular brand by any group of people who particularly attract public admiration.*'

Thursday 21 — *"Smallpox Scare"* As the World Health Organisation approaches the end of its worldwide smallpox eradication campaign, a 12-year-old British boy with suspected smallpox was admitted to a hospital in Lancashire for tests.

Friday 22 — *"Teachers Under Threat"* The government is to recommend that teachers should be dismissed in areas where the number of schoolchildren is declining.

Saturday 23 — *"Hunt for Rabies Victim"* The Department of Health are searching for a French tourist camping in southeast England, who may have rabies after being in contact with a dog in Morocco. Last month two men died in London hospitals after contracting rabies while outside Britain. The cases were the first in Britain since 1969.

Sunday 24 — *"Asleep at The Wheel"* A 30ft yacht was found by the Torbay lifeboat, drifting through shipping lanes in the Channel with the lone crew member of the Swedish vessel sound asleep. He was sailing from the West Indies to Sweden.

Monday 25 — *"Anger at Commons Deal"* MPs are complaining after learning that a £12,000 order for tableware for the House of Commons has been placed with a West German company. British manufacturers were not even asked to tender.

Tuesday 26 — *"Hoax on Gas Rigs"* 60 men were evacuated to Great Yarmouth and gas supplies shut down after a call said that bombs had been attached to the legs of one of the rigs. Divers braved dangerous currents in the North Sea searching for them but found nothing.

HERE IN BRITAIN

"Soviet Village Saved"

A British Post Office Engineer was presented with a bravery certificate and cheque for £150 by the PO for preventing a serious accident in the Soviet Union, where he was part of a team taking special telephone cabling vehicles to an exhibition in Moscow.

He said *"I pulled up in this village. Opened the shutters at the back of the lorry and thick smoke poured out. It must have been smouldering for about two and a half hours."* He quickly drove the lorry containing butane gas cylinders and other inflammable material away.

AROUND THE WORLD

"Balloon Crossing Fails"

A Trans-Atlantic crossing by the American balloonist, Robert Sparks, failed because of a helium leak. However, the flight was doomed from the start. A ground crew member wanted to become famous and had stowed away on the balloon and had tampered with the rip line so the balloon could not be deflated once he was discovered. The balloon was forced down 125 miles south-east of Cape Cod, and Sparks was taken off by helicopter, leaving the 'stowaway' to guard the balloon's gondola before being rescued this morning by a Coast Guard cutter.

Edinburgh Fringe Festival

The population of Edinburgh almost doubled in size as visitors flocked to the capital for the annual summer Festival this month, which many would argue is the best time to visit Edinburgh as the city becomes the centre of the entertainment world. Visitors and locals alike are treated to performances in the arts, music, theatre, dance, comedy, and literature.

The Fringe started life when eight theatre companies turned up uninvited to the inaugural Edinburgh International Festival in 1947. With all the city's major venues in use, these companies took over smaller, alternative venues for their productions. It is an open access performing arts festival, meaning that there is no selection committee, and anyone may participate, with any type of performance. The official Fringe Programme categorises shows into sections for theatre, comedy, dance, theatre, circus, cabaret, children's shows, musicals, opera, music, spoken word, exhibitions, and events. Comedy is the largest section, making up over one-third of the programme, and the one that in modern times has the highest public profile.

The Edinburgh Festival has not only attracted big names like Maria Callas, Richard Burton and Donald Pleasence, but has become the springboard for many careers. Robin Williams first appeared at the Edinburgh Fringe in 1971 in a production of "The Taming of the Shrew" before going on to be a huge name on both sides of the Atlantic. Peter Cook, who became one of the leading figures in the satire boom of the 60's, first appeared here with Dudley Moore, Alan Bennet and Jonathan Miller in 'Beyond The Fringe'. The Cambridge Footlights Revue appear regularly and have introduced us to actors who have gone on to star in television and cinema such as John Cleese, and Emma Thompson.

AUG 27TH - SEPT 2ND 1975

IN THE NEWS

Wednesday 27 — **"Train Robber Jailed Again"** Ronald 'Buster' Edwards, released on parole less than five months ago, was given six months for shoplifting four women's shirts, a pair of pliers and two packets of staples from Harrods.

Thursday 28 — **"Pupil's Choice"** A report by the Scottish Council of the Labour Party, on school truancy, suggests pupils should choose their own teachers. It stated that truants chose specific times to stay away, to avoid subjects and teachers they disliked.

Friday 29 — **"Bomb in Oxford Street"** Seven people were injured when a bomb exploded in Oxford Street after a telephone warning call was made to 'The Sun' newspaper. The blast happened within 24 hours of a pub bomb in Surrey which injured 11 people.

Saturday 30 — **"State Funeral Plans"** Eamon de Valera, former Eire President, has died aged 92. His body will lie in state at Dublin Castle followed by a National Day of Mourning throughout the Irish Republic to mark the day of his funeral.

Sunday 31 — **"Royal Tap"** A telephone engineer has admitted he is the Post Office employee who resigned after security inquiries into 'nuisance' calls to Princess Anne's home at Sandhurst. He says he listened to calls but denied speaking. He has accused The Post Office of making him the scapegoat, *'They have made me take all the blame.'*

Mon Sept 1 — **"Channel Victor Swims On"** An Evening Standard journalist became the first person to have twice completed the double crossing of the Channel, and then immediately set off on the third crossing. His first leg took just over 36 hours, as he battled the tides.

Tuesday 2 — **"Not in The Front"** A senior pathologist has called for new laws to stop children travelling in the front passenger seat of a car. *"Even on a mother's lap they run a very considerable risk of death or serious injury in an accident."*

HERE IN BRITAIN

"Tandem Record Journey"

British couple, Colin and Veronica Scargill seem to be perfectly matched when it comes to spending their leisure time. They bought their first tandem bicycle shortly after they were married four years ago. Colin has always been a stronger cyclist than Veronica, so it made sense to combine their efforts.

They have toured extensively throughout Britain, but this year they have just completed an 18,020km Round The World trip, breaking the record for a journey by tandem bike.

AROUND THE WORLD

"Kissinger Upstaged"

Elizabeth Taylor and Richard Burton arrived from Zurich, at Ben Gurion airport outside Tel Aviv. They are in Jerusalem to make a film and stole the show from the American Secretary of State, Dr Henry Kissinger.
Before they arrived at the King David I Hotel, whose historic guests have included Sir Winston Churchill and King Farouk, the star guest, Dr Kissinger, and his party had taken over the entire sixth floor. However once the Burtons were ensconced in rooms 228, 229 and 230, the talk was of nothing else!

Notting Hill Carnival

Notting Hill Carnival from 1975 to the 21st Century

Carnival isn't new to British culture. Bartholomew and Southward Fairs in the 18th century were moments of great festivity, with juggling, pick pocketing, whoring, drinking, and masquerade. However, all that stopped during the Puritans rule of Oliver Cromwell and was never really re-established until the 1960's, when a move to ease inter-racial tensions in London brought it to life again. Now, each year on August bank holiday weekend, the streets of Notting Hill in West London are transformed by the world's second largest, and Europe's largest, street carnival.

Those who settled in Notting Hill faced racism and violence, however local activist Rhaune Laslett felt not enough was being done to bring the community together. In a bid for integration, she organised Notting Hill Fayre and Pageant in 1966 where a steel band drew a crowd as they roamed through the streets. There was never supposed to be a procession, but one year, one of the steel drum bands impulsively went for a wander, and since then, the route has changed and expanded considerably.

By the 1970s, Caribbean masquerade traditions provided the mesmerising costumes, while soca, calypso, dub and reggae gave carnival its thumping soundtrack. The 1973 carnival, organised by Leslie Palmer, was a significant turning point. More masks and costumes were worn, some designed by experienced masquerade-makers from Trinidad. There were 70 stages, 300 food stalls and an estimated 30 million sequins. The costumes allow the wearer to disguise themselves and take on a different character. Every year, mass bands gather to create and coordinate their costumes as a group, each choosing their own theme and competing for prizes.

Sept 3rd – 9th 1975

IN THE NEWS

Wednesday 3 — **"Restaurant Chain in Liquidation"** 'London Eating Houses', a leading restaurant chain and one of the largest Wimpy bar franchisees has stopped trading and 800 employees will be made redundant.

Thursday 4 — **"Hooligans Force Prices Up"** To combat hooliganism, British Rail will no longer sell any cheap day tickets on Saturdays before 3 pm, and all football specials trains are being withdrawn. Recently passengers have been terrorised and carriages damaged.

Friday 5 — **"London Hilton Bombed"** Two people were killed and 62 injured when a bomb exploded on the ground floor of the Hilton Hotel, in the West End of London. A warning had been telephoned to a newspaper office.

Saturday 6 — **"Motorway Noise"** People living near the M5 and A14 in the South-west are to have double-glazing installed by the Government's Property Services Agency, at a cost of more than £55,000, in an attempt to reduce traffic noise in the residential areas.

Sunday 7 — **"Chips May Cost More"** The poor potato harvest has caused a trebling of prices to food processors. Birds Eye Foods are already looking to increase the cost of frozen chips again, after only 10 days since the last price rise.

Monday 8 — **"Charity Stamps"** The charity postage stamp experiment, whereby 4½p stamps were sold at 6p with the 1½p extra going to charities, will not be repeated because of the high administration costs. Last month of the £84,000 raised, only 45% went to charity.

Tuesday 9 — **"Scotland Ban"** Billy Bremner, captain of Scotland and Leeds United, and four other international football players have been suspended from playing for Scotland for life, after they were ejected from a Copenhagen night-club for rowdy behaviour.

HERE IN BRITAIN

"Buy British"

The British motor industry has been criticised for buying car components from foreign manufacturers. There were no British locks, door handles or boot latches on any of British Leyland current models, all were being supplied by foreign firms.

In the engine, the British Joseph Lucas name is on most of the electrical equipment, but at least 50% of the parts are produced in Japan or Hong Kong, using the Lucas name. *'If we want a British car, it should be a British car and not a British built car with foreign parts'.*

AROUND THE WORLD

"Assassination Attempt Failed"

President Ford survived an assassination attempt in Sacramento, California, when a woman aimed a loaded pistol at him. A bodyguard quickly subdued her before the gun could be fired. The woman shouted repeatedly, *'It didn't go off'* as she was wrestled to the ground.

Less than 90 minutes later, Ford delivered a speech on crime and gun control to the California State Legislature, not mentioning the attack. Later, the President said the attempt would not stop him from engaging with the American people.

Protected Inns

The Ye Olde Trip To Jerusalem in Nottingham, The Angel Posting House in Guildford and the Three Swans in Market Harborough.

The British 'pub' is an institution that has been part of our heritage for many generations, some dating back to the late Middle Ages, and their architecture and interiors add to the colourful backdrop of English towns and villages, which is why many have been given 'protected status' from The Brewers' Society. This means that no alterations to the fabric or décor of the building can be made without permission from the society.

Guildford's steep and cobbled High Street has five scheduled inns, including the 'Angel', a fine old coaching inn with a 600-year-old cellar and the 'Lion', where Pepys's writes that *'he cut for himself the best asparagus he had eaten in his life'*.

The 'Old Salutation' and the 'Trip to Jerusalem' at Nottingham are included and both claim to be among the oldest of English inns. Local tradition holds that the 'Trip to Jerusalem', built into the caverns hewed from the rock on which Nottingham Castle stands, received its name because it was used by soldiers going to the crusades. At Exeter the 'Ship' and the 'Turk's Head' are on the list. The Ship boasts a copy of a letter said to have been written in 1587 by Drake, in which he said, "*Next to mine own ship I do most dearly love that old Ship in Exon*," and continues with news of the sailing of the Armada. At the Turk's Head Charles Dickens is said to have started to write 'Pickwick Papers'.

Other inns mentioned include the 'Three Swans' at Market Harborough, which was well established in the sixteenth century and became the headquarters of both sides in the Civil War a century later and the Swan at Bedford, built in 1794 and containing a seventeenth-century staircase. The Brewers' Society intends eventually to mark the protected inns with a special plaque.

SEPT 10TH-16TH 1975

IN THE NEWS

Wednesday 10 — **"Needles for Nation"** The National Trust has been given the money to buy the Needles headland, on the Isle of Wight. The old MOD installations will have to be demolished before the public can be allowed access.

Thursday 11 — **"Bell Bottoms Go"** The Royal Navy's traditional uniform for junior ratings is to be changed. The bell bottoms, black kerchief, lanyard and tapes will be replaced with a more modern design approved by the Queen.

Friday 12 — **"Shutdown After Midnight"** BBC Radio 2 will close at midnight on weekdays, leaving only Radio 3's Open University programmes and commercial radio for listeners after 12am.

Saturday 13 — **"Tartan Army Claims"** Police are investigating claims that the Tartan Army, an extremist group responsible for two previous attacks on pylons carrying electricity from Scotland to England, blew up a BP oil pipeline in Tayside.

Sunday 14 — **"Soviet Shadows"** Russian 'spy' trawlers shadowed the US Navy's nuclear task group as it sailed to Portsmouth. *"Right off the English Channel the fishing fleet is not British, but Soviet. I do not think the public realise what has happened,"* the US Commander said.

Monday 15 — **"Roman Site Threatened"** One of the best-preserved Roman town sites in Britain at Alcester, near Stratford on Avon, scheduled as an ancient monument since 1962, faces destruction by developers after its protected status was unaccountably omitted from the latest local housing plan.

Tuesday 16 — **"Jensen Cars in Trouble"** Despite recently launching a GT version of the Jensen Healey, the Midlands specialist car manufacturer has called in a receiver. Management blames union difficulties and inflation for its financial problems.

HERE IN BRITAIN
"Johnny Go Home"

Yorkshire TV documentary 'Johnny Go Home' shocked the nation this week with its portrait of teenage runaways forced into prostitution in cities such as London. Part one, 'The End of the Line' followed the case histories of Tommy, a 12 year-old boy, and Annie, a 16 year-old girl, hardened to her homelessness.

The second 'The Murder of Billy Two-Tone' forensically uncovered the facts behind the killing of Billy McPhee, revealing that the owner of a homeless children's hostel was a child sex abuser whose empire was based on sexual exploitation and financial corruption.

AROUND THE WORLD
"Rembrandt Painting Slashed"

Rembrandt's painting *'The Night Watch'* was slashed by a man with a bread knife who fought off a museum guard and claimed he *'did it for the Lord.'* The attacker arrived shortly after the Rijksmuseum's afternoon opening, heading straight to the painting and slashing its lower centre.

The attacker made over a dozen deep cuts, severely damaging a seven-foot section of the 14' x 11' canvas. The damage is significant, but not irreparable, and restoration is expected to take at least four months. This was the second knife attack on the painting in recent years.

THE PILGRIM FATHERS

In early September 1620, a group of English Puritan families, seeking freedom from religious persecution, left England for America to find a new life. Originally planning to reach America by early October, delays reduced their two-ship plan to just *The Mayflower*. Departing from Southampton, the ship's provisions were already low, and further delays only made things worse. The cramped, uncomfortable quarters on the small cargo ship were ill-suited for the 102 passengers, who faced a taxing two-month journey.

The Mayflower was considered a small cargo ship, not an ocean vessel, and was in poor condition and in fact was sold for scrap just four years after her voyage. The passengers, packed closely together, believed they had a 'covenant like the Jewish people of old' and viewed America as their new Promised Land. The first part of the voyage was calm, but storms soon struck, battering the ship with continuous north-easterly winds and heavy waves. During one storm, William Butten, an indentured servant, died - the only fatality of the journey – and a baby, Oceanus Hopkins, was also born on board. In another violent storm, *The Mayflower* was forced to drift without sails for days to avoid losing her masts. Passengers crouched in darkness below deck, holding onto each other as waves tossed the ship. Despite the harsh conditions, the ship's cargo included essential supplies, tools, food, weapons, and live animals such as dogs, sheep, and goats and they eventually made landfall on November 21st.

Today the voyage of the Pilgrim Fathers is commemorated by memorials in both Southampton, Hampshire, where a Portland Stone column faces out to sea, and also in Plymouth, Massachusetts, which faces out roughly in the direction of England, a testament to Anglo-American friendship and to perpetuate the memory of the Pilgrim Fathers.

Sept 17th - 23rd 1975

IN THE NEWS

Wednesday 17 — **"Housewives in Need"** According to the National Consumer Congress, many husbands keep their pay rises to themselves, and others pass less than half to their wives for housekeeping. With rising prices, barely more than one fifth of housewives manage.

Thursday 18 — **"Price Surveys Grants"** Shirley Williams, Minister for Prices and Consumer Protection approved six local price comparison schemes which will collect and publish the prices of basic foods and household items at major supermarkets.

Friday 19 — **"Pattie Hearst Arrested"** The newspaper heiress, hunted by the FBI for over a year, has been arrested in San Francisco. These arrests end the saga which began in 1974 with her kidnapping by the Symbionese Liberation Army.

Saturday 20 — **"Lloyd George Letters"** Previous Prime Minister David Lloyd George and his mistress, Frances Stevenson, were lovers for just over 30 years until she became his second wife in 1943. Their intimate correspondence appears for the first time in The Sunday Times in extracts from the book *'My Darling Pussy'*

Sunday 21 — **"Film Influence"** A mother blamed the film, *'The Towering Inferno'*, for her 16-year-old son's fire-raising actions, claiming it influenced him. He admitted setting fires to two schools and churches in Kirkcaldy.

Monday 22 — **"Rollers Hurt"** Stuart Wood, guitarist with the Bay City Rollers pop group, was knocked unconscious for several minutes when hysterical fans rushed past security guards and overpowered the group at the London Weekend television studio.

Tuesday 23 — **"Crash Helmet Protest"** 500 Sikhs marched through Slough protesting about a colleague's jail sentence for refusing to pay a £50 fine for twice riding his motorcycle wearing his turban instead of a crash helmet.

HERE IN BRITAIN

"Fawlty Towers"

This week, the BBC aired the first episode of Fawlty Towers, the British sitcom written by John Cleese and Connie Booth. Set in the dysfunctional Fawlty Towers hotel, the character of 'Basil Fawlty', the fictional owner, was inspired when John Cleese stayed at the Gleneagles Hotel, Torquay, in 1970, and encountered the eccentric owner, Donald Sinclair who treated guests 'as though they were a hindrance to his running of the hotel - a waitress who worked for him stated *'it was as if he didn't want the guests to be there'*.

AROUND THE WORLD

"Floating Clinics"

Two Italian luxury liners, *'The Michelangelo'* and *'The Raffael'*, have been sold to a West German company for use as floating clinics for the medical study of cancerous tumours.

It is understood that the buyers have paid approximately 11.2m Euros for the liners, and that the work of adapting and reordering them to their new purpose will be carried out in Italian shipyards, and once completed they are expected to sail with predominantly Italian crews.

Last Night Of The Proms

There have been Promenade Concerts – literally, concerts where you can walk about, in London, for more than a hundred years and our present series can trace its ancestry to the entertainments in the public gardens of Vauxhall, Ranelagh and Marylebone in the eighteenth century. The original English promenade concerts at the Lyceum Theatre in 1838 were conducted by Musard and consisted of instrumental music of a light character, containing overtures, solos for a wind instrument and dance music (quadrilles and waltzes).

The change from theatre to concert hall, Queen's Hall, was made by Robert Newman when, in 1895, he started the present series with Henry J Wood as conductor. Newman wished to generate a wider audience for concert hall music by offering low ticket prices and an informal atmosphere, where eating, drinking and smoking were allowed. He said, "I am going to run nightly concerts and train the public by easy stages. Popular at first, gradually raising the standard until I have created a public for classical and modern music."

In 1927, the BBC saw that taking the concerts on would provide a full season for broadcast and would fulfil the Corporation's remit to 'inform, educate and entertain'. After the Queen's Hall was bombed in 1941 the Proms moved to the Albert Hall where their policy remains, classics plus new works and among the established artists, promising newcomers. This year's season started on 25th July with Gustav Mahler's Symphony No 8 in E flat major, 'Symphony of a Thousand' and finished, with much flag waving and cheering, on 20th September with William Walton's 'Portsmouth Point' and the traditional 'Pomp and Circumstance March - Land of Hope and Glory' by Edward Elgar.

Sept 24th - 30th 1975

IN THE NEWS

Wednesday 24 — **"Headlights At Night"** New regulations proposed for this autumn when the clocks go back, will oblige motorists to use headlights at night whether or not the road is lit.

Thursday 25 — **"Learner Driver Banned"** A learner-driver in Leeds was jailed for six months and banned for seven years after four incidents in five months of driving well over the alcohol limit. The magistrate said, *'I cannot imagine how you have got away without killing yourself or someone else'.*

Friday 26 — **"First Britons"** Dougal Haston and Doug Scott have not only become the first British climbers to reach the summit of Everest, but also the first to do so by the difficult route up the South-West face which has defeated five previous international expeditions.

Saturday 27 — **"Glove Print Method"** A method of detecting and identifying prints left by criminals wearing gloves has been perfected by Scotland Yard detectives. The method claims to be almost as reliable as the fingerprint system.

Sunday 28 — **"Home Tobacco Scheme"** Two tobacco companies are experimenting with tobacco grown in Britain. If they are successful and the products popular, they hope to avoid import duties levied as a result of Britain's EEC membership.

Monday 29 — **"Spaghetti House Siege"** Gunmen claiming to represent the 'Black Liberation Front' held seven Italians hostage in a Knightsbridge restaurant after releasing one. Police surrounded the building following a staff member's escape.

Tuesday 30 — **"Slim is Healthy"** A campaign has been launched advising mothers to breastfeed to help keep babies slim. They say that fat babies often grow into fat children and adults, increasing the risk of diabetes, heart disease, and other conditions.

HERE IN BRITAIN

"New Shrub Escapes Thief's Hand"

At the Royal Horticultural Society's autumn show in London, a new, vivid scarlet variety of Potentilla fruticosa, - shrubby cinquefoil - named 'Red Ace,' was awarded a first-class certificate and a plant patent applied for, due to its propagation potential.

A visitor was caught 'red handed' taking a cutting of this 'most remarkable advance for many years' prompting organisers to remove the plant from the show. Safeguarding plant breeders' rights is crucial, as one stolen cutting could quickly be propagated and ruin the breeder's expected significant profits.

AROUND THE WORLD

"Goodbye Singapore"

The frigate Mermaid steamed ceremoniously out of Singapore, ending a British naval presence there which had lasted for a century and a half. The ship, sailed into the sunset to the sound of the pipes and drums of the 1st battalion, the Gordon Highlanders, bound for a final farewell tour of the region.

The Gordon Highlanders themselves are also in the process of leaving Singapore and the RAF Nimrod maritime patrol aircraft have already departed. The few remaining helicopters will go soon and by next March the last British serviceman should have left.

MICHAELMAS DAY

Nottingham Goose Fair (main). A goose market (inset).

The Feast of Michael and All Angels Day, known as Michaelmas, was celebrated on the 29th September with religious ceremonies up and down the country. The day traditionally marks the beginning of Autumn and the official shortening of days, marking one of the four 'quarter days' in England. *Lady Day* in March, *Midsummer* in June, *Michaelmas* in September and *Christmas* in December make up the four 'quarter days' in traditional British folklore; spaced three months apart, the days all typically hold religious meaning and fall near an equinox or a solstice. It was on these days that servants were hired or fired, rent was collected and leases were signed. Michaelmas was originally particularly important, as it marked the end of the harvest season, but this became less so following the split from the Catholic Church under Henry VIII in the early 1530s, when the *Harvest Festival* was celebrated a few weeks later on October 10th.

Thousands of families across Britain feasted on a well fattened goose to, according to tradition, protect against financial need in the family for the next year: *'Eat a goose on Michaelmas Day, want not for money all the year.'* Because of this, Michaelmas has earned the nickname *'Goose Day'* and the famous Nottingham Goose fair is still held on the weekend closest to the festival. It stems from a rumour that goose was the food being eaten by Queen Elizabeth I upon hearing of the defeat of the Spanish Armada in 1588, vowing to finish the bird on Michaelmas in celebration.

In British folklore, Michaelmas is the last time that blackberries should be picked, as it was on this day that Lucifer was expelled from heaven, landing on a prickly blackberry bush, and proceeding to scorch it with fiery breath.

Oct 1st – 7th 1975

IN THE NEWS

Wednesday 1 — **"Pre-Roman Settlement"** Evidence of a pre-Roman settlement in London has been discovered in the City, on the north bank of the Thames, with pottery and flint tools dating to 1400 BC.

Thursday 2 — **"Terror Attacks in Ulster"** Eleven people died and at least 30 were injured, mostly Roman Catholics, in attacks on six pubs. This savage outbreak of sectarian violence in Ulster has raised fears of an outbreak of full civil war.

Friday 3 — **"Oops!"** A London property developer is on trial at Brighton Magistrates Court, charged with demolishing a wall of the town's 16th century Black Lion Brewery without planning permission. The Black Lion brewery was established by a Flemish immigrant, the first Protestant to be martyred under Mary I.

Saturday 4 — **"Strict Labelling for Yogurt"** The Food Standards Committee is campaigning for stricter rules for labelling yoghurt. Manufacturers should not call un-flavoured yogurt "natural" just to distinguish it from yoghurt with added fruit.

Sunday 5 — **"Re-opening Stations"** A combination of public demand and British Rail rethinking has produced the impetus to reopen railway stations that have been disused for a decade or more. *'The little lines brought business to the main ones,'* British Rail admits.

Monday 6 — **"Dearer Mail and Slower"** Since postal charges increased, some second-class mail is taking a day longer to deliver and is being posted without stamps. The slower service was one of four economies agreed as an alternative to even higher increases.

Tuesday 7 — **"Mine Sweeping Hovercraft"** A Royal Navy bomb disposal team used a hovercraft for the first time to search for unexploded WWII bombs on the Essex marshes. A number were found, together with a part of a Dakota transport aircraft.

HERE IN BRITAIN

"London Crime Wave"

A crime wave hit London as 300 crime writers gathered for the first international congress at the Piccadilly Hotel, organised by Penelope Wallace, daughter of Edgar Wallace. Attendees include seasoned mystery authors, from genteel writers to action-genre Americans, discussing their craft.

Experts like Sir Robert Mark and Professor H. J. Eysenck will speak on real-life crime, with papers on locks, lock-picking, and firearms. The main focus will be networking among writers, exchanging clues and ideas.

AROUND THE WORLD

"He is The Greatest"

Muhammad Ali retained his world heavyweight boxing title when Joe Frazier's corner stopped the fight in the 14th round. The 'Thrilla in Manila' as the event was dubbed, was televised from the Philippines and streamed around the world.

The fight was watched by around 1 billion people worldwide. This included 100 million viewers on closed-circuit television and 500,000 pay-per-view buys on HBO. Ali won by technical knockout (TKO) and then collapsed with exhaustion after being pronounced the winner.

WELSH STRUGGLES

Once there was the curious tale of an inn which straddled a wet-dry border. On Sundays the public bar was dry and empty, but the lounge bar was wet and crowded.

As pub opening time approaches on Sundays, some men in Wales still walk, or even drive, across the county boundaries to get their Sunday pint. Or they belong to clubs. Or they may even go for a ride in the buffet car of the Ffestiniog railway, which is a thin, wet line in a Sunday-dry Gwynedd. *'It really is a ridiculous situation,'* said the hotelier chairman of the Seven Day Opening Council, *'Day visitors to Wales who walk into an hotel will see guests drinking at the bar, but they themselves, not being guests, cannot be served. We aim to remove this anachronism and make all of Wales wet on Sundays.'*

he secretary of The Temperance Committee of the Baptist Church Union of Wales, said, *'The figures for alcoholism and absenteeism are increasing. Wales would be better off if people drank less or gave it up. And as far as Sunday is concerned, we regard it as a special day and, as the last poll showed, people of five counties wanted to keep the old tradition.'* Therefore, in pulpit and public bar, in manse and hotel lounge, the battle plans are being drawn up. On one side, in the fastnesses of Welsh Wales, are the last defenders of that once mighty Welsh institution, the quiet family Sunday unstained by alcohol. On the other, and growing in strength, are licensees, the drinking classes and plain citizens who maintain that the Welshman's right to a Sunday pint, to say 'Iechyd da' (good health) to his friends in all parts of Wales, should no longer be denied. Dwyfor was the last district to allow Sunday opening in 1996.

Oct 8th - 14th 1975

IN THE NEWS

Wednesday 8 — **"Charles in Command"** The Prince of Wales, now a Lieutenant in the Royal Navy and a qualified helicopter pilot, is to be given his first command. HMS Bronington is a 300-ton Rosyth-based mine hunter.

Thursday 9 — **"Beefalo Bull"** The first British supplies of meat from a cow/American bison cross, called a 'beefalo', will soon be sold in our butchers' shops. It will give leaner cuts and cost only a quarter the price of beef.

Friday 10 — **"Electric Taxi"** Lucas Industries have developed Britain's first battery powered taxi. With a speed of 55 mph and a range of 100 miles per charge. They are 40 inches shorter than the present London taxi but have the same turning circle and more room inside and are almost silent and free of pollution.

Saturday 11 — **"Pilots Warning"** Trainee airline pilots have been informed that excessive smoking is a high-risk health indicator. The pilot of the future will ideally be a non-smoker or restrict their consumption to five cigarettes a day.

Sunday 12 — **"Not So Sweet Tooth"** Manufacturers report that the consumption of sweets in Britain has fallen by a tenth since last year, but that hasn't prevented the cost of sweets sold from rising by more than 25%.

Monday 13 — **"Fireworks Ban"** With Guy Fawkes night coming up, the National Campaign for Firework Reform claims most people want fireworks banned, stricter controls over their retail sale or limited to licensed events.

Tuesday 14 — **"Squatters Loan"** Public opinion in the London borough of Tower Hamlets is divided over a proposal to lend a group of squatters about £500,000 to buy and renovate the block of council flats they have taken over.

HERE IN BRITAIN

"Conker Championships"

64 contenders entered the 11th World Conker Championships in Northamptonshire. Players from around the world competed in a knock-out format in both team and individual formats.

The event began in 1965 when a group of anglers held a conker contest at the local pub when the weather was too bad to go fishing. At the event, a small collection was made for charity, since then the event has raised money for visually impaired people, with at least £2,500 donated yearly.

AROUND THE WORLD

"Imperial Visit To San Francisco"

Emperor Hirohito and Empress Nagako Kuni are visiting Washington D.C. following the Japan-United States Friendship Act of 1975. On arrival, the imperial motorcade stopped at Golden Gate Park's Botanical Garden where the emperor gave a short speech.
He then laid a wreath at the Tomb of the Unknowns - the memorial in the Arlington National Cemetery to unknown Americans brought home from WW2 battlefields for burial. The emperor also visited Disneyland, where he was given a Mickey Mouse watch.

Hollywood Walk Of Fame

To mark his fifth US number one single, 'Island Girl', Elton John has received a star on the Hollywood Walk of Fame. This landmark which consists of 2,800 five-pointed stars embedded in the sidewalks along 15 blocks of Hollywood Boulevard and three blocks of Vine Street in Los Angeles is a popular tourist attraction. The historic Hollywood Hotel, which stood for more than 50 years on Hollywood Boulevard, displayed stars on its dining room ceiling above the tables favoured by its most famous celebrity patrons, and that may have served as an early inspiration.

The coral-pink terrazzo five-point stars, spaced at 6-foot intervals, are mostly monuments to achievement in the entertainment industry, each bearing the name of the recipient in brass. Below the inscription, a brass symbol indicates the honouree's contribution to one of the six categories: Films, Television, Music, Radio, Theatre or Broadcasting, but, the plaques for the Apollo 11 Mission to the Moon are uniquely shaped, showing circular moons, each bearing the name of Neil Armstrong, Edwin Aldrin, and Michael Collins. Muhammad Ali's star is the only star mounted on a wall, granting Ali's request that his name not be walked upon, as he shared his name with the Islamic prophet Muhammad.

So many fans were wanting to see Elton John that the organisers, for the first time ever, had to close the actual opening ceremony to the public, who were kept behind a rope barricade. John wore a diamanté trimmed suit and bowler hat, with star shaped lenses in his spectacles, and with deadpan humour announced *"I am pleased to declare this supermarket open ….. oh sorry, wrong place….."* before his star was unveiled.

OCT 15TH - 21TH 1975

IN THE NEWS

Wednesday 15 — **"Sold Out"** Tickets for the first Concorde flights went on sale with the first three journeys fully booked, from a register of people which has been kept over the past 11 years.

Thursday 16 — **"Burtons Reunited"** Divorced only last year, Richard Burton and Elizabeth Taylor have now remarried in a village in the Botswana bush.

Friday 17 — **"Jumble Sale Bowl"** A French silver-gilt bowl, bought at a Sidcup, Kent, jumble sale for 80p fetched £9,000 at Sotheby's. Turns out it was a rare French piece of the reign of Louis XIV dated 1686.

Saturday 18 — **"US Dim Hopes for Concorde"** A decision by the United States on whether to permit Concorde to use Dulles International airport in Washington is to be delayed while new data from an official report on its high noise levels at Heathrow airport, are studied.

Sunday 19 — **"Anti-Abortion Rally"** The abortion debate reached an emotional climax with a rally of more than 50,000 people in Hyde Park, London, organised by the Society for the Protection of Unborn Children. When the subsequent procession reached Whitehall, it was met by about 150 counter demonstrators, most members of the 'A Woman's Right to Choose' campaign.

Monday 20 — **"Roof Garden to Stay"** The Biba store in Kensington High Street has closed after only two years of trading. However, a preservation order has been placed on the roof garden.

Tuesday 21 — **"Ferry Crew Release Cars"** Seamen on board the strike bound car-passenger ferry 'Eagle', accepted an offer from their employers the P&O shipping company, and agreed to release the 40 cars which had been trapped on the ferry at Southampton for five days.

HERE IN BRITAIN

"Everest Man Left Behind"

An Everest team defended their decision not to wait for BBC cameraman Michael Burke, who died attempting a solo summit. Expedition leader Chris Bonington said, *"It was 100% the right decision. Only one man lost his life—three would have died if they stayed."*
Peter Boardman and Sherpa Pertember had reached the summit and were descending when they encountered Burke, who was about 10-15 minutes from the top and insisted to continue alone. Despite waiting an hour for him, worsening weather conditions forced the climbers to descend without him.

AROUND THE WORLD

"Vigilant Paris Cleaner Foils Bomb Plot"

An attempt to blow up the West German cultural institute in Paris was foiled by a vigilant woman cleaner and two bombs were defused in time. Shortly before the bombs were due to go off, a caller rang the Goethe Institute and said, 'Bombs are going to go off, that's from the Baader-Meinhof group'. Members of the group are on trial in Stuttgart.

The woman found the first bomb on Friday evening as she was cleaning out a rubbish bin and called the police, who searched and located a second bomb in a language classroom.

Trafalgar Day

Tuesday 21st October
Trafalgar Day Lunch

Join us to commemorate Nelson's famous victory

Trafalgar Day was marked in Britain this year with the traditional naval ceremony of colours aboard HMS Victory in Portsmouth. The white ensign and Union Jack were raised on the 150-year-old wooden galleon, before a flag sequence read Admiral Horatio Nelson's famous message to his fleet: *'England expects that every man will do his duty ...'.* Later, all over Britain the traditional Trafalgar Day Dinner was held, a grand affair with long-standing traditions including parading the baron of beef, Ship of the Line chocolate replica of the HMS Victory, reading of the historical dispatches, toasts and more.

Trafalgar Day is the annual celebration observed on October 21, commemorating the victory of the Royal Navy over the French and Spanish forces at the Battle of Trafalgar in 1805. The battle came at the height of the Napoleonic Wars, where France was the dominant European military power and were rapidly expanding under the leadership of Napoleon. Nevertheless, the Royal Navy proved that, under the command of Admiral Nelson, Britain still ruled the seas. On the Franco-Spanish front were 33-line ships, five frigates and two brigs, while the Royal Navy had just 27-line ships, four frigates, one schooner and one cutter. Despite being outnumbered, outflanked and hundreds of miles from the English Channel, Nelson employed ambitious tactics, capturing 18 French ships, and forcing Admiral Villeneuve to surrender. The British fleet he commanded consisted of warships built of wood, driven by sails, and equipped on both sides with cannons. After leading his fleet to one of the greatest maritime victories in history, Admiral Nelson died aboard HMS Victory after being hit by a Spanish musket ball. Nelson was fanned and brought lemonade and watered wine to drink and stayed alive until his deck commander confirmed the full surrender of French forces, three hours later.

Oct 22ND - 28TH 1975

IN THE NEWS

Wednesday 22 — **"Shipbuilding in Desperate Straits"** Britain's shipbuilding crisis, with thousands facing unemployment, is because of the lowest order levels in 30 years. The industry has called for urgent action and clarity on plans for nationalisation.

Thursday 23 — **"Wrong Victim"** Hugh Fraser, Tory MP, escaped harm when a bomb explosion wrecked his car parked outside his house. However, Professor Gordon Hamilton Fairley, head of the medical oncology unit at St Bartholomew's Hospital, London, and one of Britain's leading cancer experts, was passing by and was killed in the blast.

Friday 24 — **"Slow Down for Chrysler"** Chrysler's car assembly plant at Coventry, is to work only eight days in November and three days in December. The company has only been working three and four-day weeks since September.

Saturday 25 — **"Close-up of Venus"** A unique image received from a Soviet spacecraft, has indicated that Venus, Earth's closest planetary neighbour, is rocky rather than sandy.

Sunday 26 — **"Buy British"** Lincolnshire police committee has stopped their chief constable from replacing the current fleet of patrol cars with Swedish Volvo cars, as they said it was a matter of national importance to support the British motor industry.

Monday 27 — **"Rock Star Turned Sculptor"** Tommy Steele has given a statue called 'Bermondsey Boy', sculpted by himself, and based on his own likeness, to the new Rotherhithe Civic Centre which he opened officially.

Tuesday 28 — **"Finishing Bevan's Plan"** Talk of low morale in the National Health Service has been dismissed as scaremongering by Barbara Castle in the House of Commons. In phasing out pay beds she said she, *'was completing the work begun by Mr Aneurin Bevan.'*

HERE IN BRITAIN

"Anglo-American Venture"

Sir Lew Grade, chairman of Associated Television, has announced the creation of a new film company, Associated General Films. The company plans to produce 15-20 films annually, each with a budget of £3 million or more, with half of the films being made in Britain.

In partnership with General Cinema Corporation of Boston, the world's largest cinema circuit, the company aims to become the largest producer of major films. With resources of around £50 million, it will focus on "family and adventure" films for global distribution.

AROUND THE WORLD

"Women On Strike"

Icelandic women went on a one-day strike to protest about wage inequality whilst highlighting their crucial role in the economy. Working women and housewives joined the rally in Reykjavik, causing a massive traffic jam. Communications were affected due to a lack of switchboard operators; nursery schools closed, forcing some businessmen to bring children to work; women make up 100% of typesetters and newspapers were not published. Theatres closed without actresses; flights were cancelled without stewardesses and schools were disrupted as 65% of teachers are women.

Commemorative Stamps

This year has seen the publication of three sets of commemorative postage stamps. The 150th Anniversary of the first Steam Train, containing four stamps, 62nd Inter-Parliamentary Union Conference with only one stamp, and this month, the popular Jane Austen stamps which mark the bicentenary of her birth. This set has four stamps designed by Barbara Brown, depicting 'Emma', 'Northanger Abbey', 'Pride and Prejudice', and 'Mansfield Park'.

Commemorative stamps are issued on a significant date or to commemorate a place, event, person, or object. Many postal services issue several commemorative stamps each year, and they are usually printed in limited quantities and sold for a short period of time until supplies run out. Often cited as the 'world's first commemoratives' are the sixteen stamps of the United States Colombian Issue, produced to celebrate the World Colombian Exposition in 1893 in Chicago, to mark the 400th anniversary of Christopher Columbus's arrival in the New World in 1492.

Although the United Kingdom often set the standard for quality and well executed designs on postage stamps, they were later than many other countries in issuing their first commemorative stamp, which was not produced until the British Empire Commemorative set of 1924 was produced to coincide with The British Empire Exhibition. However, the appearance of commemorative stamps caused a backlash among some stamp collectors in the early years of stamp collecting, who did not relish the prospect of laying out ever-larger sums to acquire the stamps of the world. This led to the formation of the Society for the Suppression of Speculative Stamps in 1895 to blacklist these 'excessive' stamps. Nevertheless, early commemoratives are still prized by collectors, and there are many who prefer to collect the 'smaller print run' commemorative sets rather than postage sets.

Oct 29th – Nov 4th 1975

IN THE NEWS

Wednesday 29 — **"No Sunday Opening"** The Government has rejected a recommendation that public houses in Scotland should be allowed to open on Sundays but have accepted suggestions for a 'refreshment house' licence where children could accompany adults.

Thursday 30 — **"First Yorkshire Ripper Victim"** The first body was discovered in the Chapeltown district of Leeds. An extensive inquiry was embarked on, involving 150 officers of the West Yorkshire Police and 11,000 interviews.

Friday 31 — **"Disease Kills Elms"** The Forestry Commission announced that Dutch elm disease has killed more than a quarter of 1.9m elm trees in southern England.

Saturday Nov 1 — **"No Veggies Allowed"** The Vegetarian Society protested over the apparent exclusion of vegetarians from the Centre for Agricultural Strategy at Reading University. *"We resent the bar to employment of practising vegetarians in a centre that will examine the nation's agricultural needs."*

Sunday 2 — **"Stamps Withdrawn"** Guernsey has withdrawn two million special Christmas postage stamps, because postmarks can be wiped from the glossy surface, thus allowing them to be used again.

Monday 3 — **"North Sea Oil on Stream"** The Queen pressed a in button Dyce, Aberdeen, to start the flow of North Sea oil from BP's Forties field, the largest oilfield in the British sector of the North Sea. The oil is now pumping £28 a second into the economy.

Tuesday 4 — **"Free Speech"** Magistrates at Guildford were told that because of faulty equipment, dozens of people were able to make free long-distance calls by prefacing the number they wanted to dial, with a secret numerical code.

HERE IN BRITAIN

"RAF To Lose Biggin Hill"

Due to cuts in defence expenditure, Biggin Hill, the Battle of Britain fighter station, was to be removed from the RAF and offered to the Army, although The Ministry of Defence would not confirm the decision. *'Some past and present members of the RAF have come forward with an imaginative idea to turn Biggin Hill into a museum of the Battle of Britain'*, the MP for Canterbury said, *'They are confident that they can raise sufficient support to maintain the museum,'* and he has asked the Secretary of State for Defence, to stop the transfer.

AROUND THE WORLD

"Spanish Democracy"

Prince Juan Carlos, Spain's future King, has taken over from the dictator, General Franco, on a 'temporary' basis. A medical bulletin by the 19 specialists attending him said Franco's condition remained serious.

Even so, he continues to be the Chief of State for as long as he is alive. Prince Juan Carlos, who assumes power in the meantime, is the grandson of Spain's last ruling monarch, Alfonso XIII. He was proclaimed formally as the General's eventual successor and future King at a parliamentary session in 1969.

The Watercress Line

A group of dedicated volunteers have just purchased a railway line in Hampshire from British Rail, and plan to bring it back to life. The Watercress Line, now a 10-mile heritage railway, runs from Alresford to Alton and was originally opened in 1865 as the Mid-Hants Railway, but was closed in 1973.

The line originally provided an alternative route between London and Southampton and, besides transporting locally produced watercress, connected many local villages. In its Victorian heyday, most watercress farms were built either in Hampshire, Dorset or Hertfordshire where there are clear fast-flowing chalk streams, which are the vital natural habitat for wild watercress. Alresford, a beautiful Georgian town, was where the name for the Watercress Line originated, thanks to the plentiful supplies of local watercress that were shipped from there throughout the country. People have eaten watercress in Hampshire for centuries, picking it from the wild streams and ditches, however, it was too perishable to transport over poor roads, so it was not commercially grown until the arrival of the railway. The line was particularly important during both wars for military traffic between the army town of Aldershot and the military embarkation port at Southampton.

However with the development of motorised transport, the line declined during the inter-war and post-war periods, and electrification of the line from London to Alton in 1937 meant that the Watercress Line was no longer part of a through route. Further modernisation of the main line from London to Southampton via Winchester occurred in 1967, which seriously affected the economics of the Mid-Hants route and despite objections and arguments about the economics, the line eventually closed in February 1973.

Nov 5th - 11th 1975

IN THE NEWS

Wednesday 5 "Blast Furnace Explosion" Five workers died and 14 were injured by an explosion in a 190-ton ladle of molten iron at the British Steel's complex at Scunthorpe. The 40ft-high roof of the building was also ripped open by the explosion.

Thursday 6 "British Troops Flown to Belize" To deter a potential Guatemalan invasion following military activity and aggressive statements and despite reluctance from the Foreign Office, Britain has deployed troops to Belize, reinforcing the current 650-man garrison.

Friday 7 "Inveraray Castle Fire" Fire started in one of the 18th century Neo-Gothic castle's turrets, and within an hour the blaze was out of control. It's feared that £1m damage has been sustained in one of the most famous and beautifully situated castles in Scotland.

Saturday 8 "Turkey's Off" Due to the cost, the 72,000 children who stay for school lunches in Bucks., will have to have an ordinary meal instead of the traditional Christmas fare this year.

Sunday 9 "Welsh 'Wet' and 'Dry' Sundays" There is a move towards the Sunday opening of public houses in most of Wales. But in a referendum, North and West Wales, where the Welsh language and nonconformity are strong, voted to keep the Sabbath dry.

Monday 10 "Food Crisis Forecast" Rural poverty is leading to such a depletion of the farm workforce that an unprecedented food crisis is inevitable unless farm workers are paid more than the £30.50 per week they currently get.

Tuesday 11 "Penguin Takes Over American Publisher" Penguin, the British paperback publisher, have announced they are acquiring a majority interest in the American publishing house, The Viking Press.

HERE IN BRITAIN

"Stickler For Tradition"

The Prince of Wales's insistence on proposing the loyal toast after the dessert, rather than the main course, has sparked division within the Guild of Professional Toastmasters, which hopes to settle the matter at an executive meeting. Members are expected to agree that Royal Family members should be exempt from the modern practice of placing the loyal toast after the main course.

The guild president suggested the Prince "*was a bit wrong*" as the modern trend is more popular "*so that people can smoke after the main course, because people are smoking more than ever* ".

AROUND THE WORLD

"Complaining Housewives"

A debate occurred between the Polish Prime Minister and several hundred Communist Party women, complaining about the hardships faced by housewives in Poland. The televised discussion focused on the shortage and poor quality of consumer goods. The Prime Minister acknowledged the country's economic and housing challenges, admitting that many products were substandard despite using quality materials. He emphasised that the key issue was workers' attitudes toward their tasks, suggesting it would be '*ideal if each worker desired to buy the products they produced.*'

Poppy Day

57 years since the Armistice of 11 November 1918, brought the fighting in the first world war to a close the nation again commemorated the million and a half men and women who fell in two world wars. And down through the years the Act of Remembrance remains unchanged. The focus as always was the empty tomb, the Cenotaph in the middle of Whitehall, and the gathering of veterans.

The same orders of command echoed off the Government offices as they have for more than half a century. Wreaths of poppies were laid, a splash of red amongst the black and grey. This time there were two small changes appropriate for International Women's Year; for the first time a woman, Margaret Thatcher, laid a wreath as leader of the Conservative party and for the first time a woman, Dame Evelyn Dennington, Chairman of the Transport Committee of the Greater London Council, placed a wreath on behalf of the Greater London Council.

The main part in this solemn national theatre has, of course, been played by a woman for almost a quarter of a century, and the Queen performed it with her usual solemn dignity. Wreaths were laid by government and opposition members, this year Mr Callaghan, the Foreign Secretary, placed a wreath on behalf of the dead of Rhodesia. Members of the Royal Family lay theirs on behalf of the particular services or regiments they represent. The Bishop of London conducted the short service, accompanied by the boys of the choir of the Chapel Royal, in their Tudor uniforms of scarlet and gold, singing 'O God, Our Help in Ages Past'. As is tradition, there was the march past by the Royal British Legion to honour their dead comrades, their rows of medals testament to their bravery.

Nov 12th-18th 1975

IN THE NEWS

Wednesday 12 — **"Prejudicial Attacks?"** Vandals attacked 40 Volkswagen cars in a depot at Cannock, Staffordshire, causing extensive damage, whilst English cars parked there were untouched. The police said that the raid had been carefully planned.

Thursday 13 — **"Speed Limits Stay"** The temporary 50 mph and 60 mph speed limits on many roads, imposed last December as a fuel-saving measure, are to stay in place for another year.

Friday 14 — **"Catholic Funeral"** Leaders of church and state attended a requiem Mass in Westminster Cathedral for Cardinal Heenan, Archbishop of Westminster. His body was buried beneath the floor of the nave after the service.

Saturday 15 — **"Police Board Pop Music Ship"** The pop music radio station, Radio Caroline, went off the air last night after Essex police boarded its headquarters ship the 'Mia Amigo', in the Thames Estuary. Four men are to appear in court at Southend.

Sunday 16 — **"Lion Attack"** A man was attacked by a young lion, weighing more than 17 stones, and suffered scratches and shock, when he called on business at a West Midlands house. The owner, who bought the lion to protect his property, said, *'I now want to get rid of him because he has turned out to be too much trouble.'*

Monday 17 — **"Doctors Facing Showdown"** Legislation for the separation of private practice from the National Health Service, which will be outlined in the Queen's Speech, is expected to lead to open conflict within the medical profession.

Tuesday 18 — **"Navy on Trawler Patrol"** The talks on a new fishing agreement between Britain and Iceland to agree limits and net sizes, broke down, with Iceland remaining obdurate. The Royal Navy is detailing frigates for escort duties with the British fishing fleet.

HERE IN BRITAIN

"Women Lose Out"

One of the first unintended consequences of the Sex Discrimination Act emerged, as women in Liverpool lost access to cheaper train fares for shopping trips to London. British Rail had offered special 'women's day tickets', 'first-class women's executive tickets', and discounted fares for 'pairs of women'.

However, British Rail lawyers have determined these offers must end to comply with the new Act, which aims to prevent gender discrimination. Additionally, the Law means that many women's only waiting rooms at stations are also being phased out.

AROUND THE WORLD

"Galloping Inflation"

A diligent archivist in New York has discovered that New York had lent money to the Government in Washington. A loan of $1m was made for building fortifications during the war of 1812, and never repaid.

The president of New York City Council estimates that with compound interest, the federal Government now owes New York $11,200m and all because the United States declared war on Britain and her allies in June 1812, mainly because of trade restrictions introduced by Britain to impede American trade with France with which Britain was at war.

Fish Return To The Thames

Four species of fish never previously recorded in the Thames have been identified in the past three months, the Thames Water Authority have announced. The species, rock goby, allis shad, black sea bream and sandsmelt, were found during inspections at the Central Electricity Generating Board in Essex, bringing the total number of species recorded since 1964 to 87, including a hybrid. The chairman of the authority, said: *"We are very encouraged whenever we find new species."*

The Thames is considered the prime river of the nation, probably because of its location through the heart of the capital city, but it has enjoyed a chequered past down through the centuries, known more for the life on the surface of the water, than the life under the surface. Centuries of pollution from raw sewage gradually strangled the life out of the Thames, but a restoration programme with legislation started in 1961 is now beginning to show positive results.

During the 19th century the discharge of raw sewage into the Thames was common, making it a harbour for many harmful bacteria. Gasworks were built alongside the river, and their by-products leaked into the water, including spent lime, ammonia, cyanide, and carbolic acid, so that in parts, the deposit on the foreshore was more than six feet deep. The river had an unnaturally warm temperature caused by chemical reactions in the water, which also removed the water's oxygen. Four serious cholera outbreaks killed tens of thousands of people between 1832 and 1865. The stench was so bad that politicians had to close the windows of Westminster in summer to keep the smell out and Queen Victoria and Prince Albert took a pleasure cruise on the Thames, but had to return to shore within a few minutes, because the smell was so terrible!

Nov 19TH - 25TH 1975

IN THE NEWS

Wednesday 19 — **"Wreck May Be FV Gaul"** It is believed the Norwegian trawler, 'Rairo', has found the wreck of the 'Gaul', the British trawler lost without trace in the Barents Sea, Norway, in February 1974.

Thursday 20 — **"Reckless Driver"** Les McKeown, the 20-year-old lead singer of the Bay City Rollers, appeared at Edinburgh Sheriff Court charged with killing an elderly woman while driving 'recklessly' in the city. *"I didn't realise I'd hit her as I didn't feel any impact,"* he said.

Friday 21 — **"Caring Milkmen"** Under a 'care code' launched in conjunction with the Dairy Trade Federation, milkmen are to fulfil a new role to give early warnings when lonely, old or disabled people are in trouble in their homes.

Saturday 22 — **"The Undeserving Rich"** A Judge at Bedford Crown Court criticised legal aid being granted to a company director's wife convicted of shoplifting. She lives in a country mansion, has four sons at Gordonstoun, owns four fur coats and her own car.

Sunday 23 — **"Whisky Swindle"** The fraud squad and the FBI are investigating a £5m whisky scam. Tricksters sold huge consignments of bonded whisky on the understanding that it will mature and increase in value – it was, however, inferior grain, not malt, whisky.

Monday 24 — **"Hands Up!"** Christmas supermarket shoppers were advised by an MP to hold goods they have picked up from counters, over their heads, to avoid wrongful prosecution during the 'Christmas shoplifting season'.

Tuesday 25 — **"British Retreat"** British trawlers off the coast of Iceland are leaving the 200-mile zone in which Iceland have imposed a ban on foreign fishermen. This may be to await further developments rather than for good.

HERE IN BRITAIN
"Women Reprieved"

Threatened only last week by the new Sex Discrimination Act, women's waiting rooms have been reprieved. British Railways have decided to change its mind about abolishing them, as women's waiting rooms usually have lavatories attached, so they would win exemption on the ground of necessary 'decency or privacy'.

This would also cover providing facilities for nursing mothers who would be in a state of undress and thus entitled to privacy. When asked why they wanted to keep women's waiting rooms, women invariably reply, *"In order not to be bothered by men "*.

AROUND THE WORLD
"Franco Buried"

A granite slab weighing more than a ton and a half sealed off the chief protagonist of nearly half a century of Spanish history. General Franco was buried at the colossal mausoleum he built over 18 years, the Valley of the Fallen, in the Guadarrama mountains, 35 miles from Madrid.

His wooden coffin with a carved crucifix was lowered into the tomb behind the high altar in the huge basilica, which forms a part of the complex. Previously, 20,000 people had queued for hours to pass his bier, laid out at the Oriente Palace.

Beaujolais Nouveau

This British charity event was hatched on the 18th November, 1970 over a dinner of coq au vin in the hotel Maritonnes, shared by friends Clement Freud and Joseph Berkmann. Owner of eight London restaurants, Berkmann also ran a wine distribution company and wrote a weekly column for The Sunday Times. Clement Freud was Director of the London Playboy Club, a Liberal MP and wine correspondent for The Sun.

Over several bottles of wine that evening, this jolly wheeze of an idea took shape and sometime after midnight, they roared away from Romanèche in France, with several cases of Beaujolais in the back of each car, having challenged each other to be the first to get their cases back to London. For two years the race was a private event between them, with Berkmann winning both times and much joshing took place in their respective columns, until eventually, word got around that something interesting was going on, and 'The Beaujolais Race' was begun. In 1973, Sunday Times columnist, Alan Hall, delivered the challenge to 'Bring Back the Beaujolais', offering a bottle of Champagne for the first team to deliver a bottle of the new vintage to his desk.

The winner this year was John Patterson, the owner of 'Tiles Restaurant' in London, plonking a case of 1975 Beaujolais Primeur on Hall's desk at 2.30 am, just three and a half hours after leaving Burgundy. He flew the wine over in a Cessna 310 light aircraft to Gatwick, winning by only a few seconds because he was lucky enough to find the front door of The Sunday Times open for the cleaners. The runners-up, Peter Dominic's Wine Mine Club, also used a Cessna 310, but landed at Heathrow and used the newspaper's back door.

Nov 26th – Dec 2nd 1975

IN THE NEWS

Wednesday 26 — **"Firework Control"** Firework sales will be restricted to those over 16, available only for three weeks before and three days after Bonfire Night. 'Flyabout' fireworks are banned, with increased penalties for violations.

Thursday 27 — **"Island Post Warning"** Industrial action by Guernsey harbour workers is severely delaying parcel post to and from the island. The Post Office has advised customers not to post parcels to Guernsey containing perishable goods.

Friday 28 — **"You Can't Beat the Budget"** The Home Office has authorised 4,000 letters to be sent out, warning that 'overlapping' colour television licences taken out to beat the April Budget increases, will be revoked.

Saturday 29 — **"Terrorists Should Forfeit Right to Life"** Mrs Thatcher, Leader of the Opposition, stated her belief that the death penalty should be restored for terrorist murders, while acknowledging that each MP must make a personal decision on the matter.

Sunday 30 — **"Royal Expenses Scrutiny"** The new Civil List Bill alters the system of annual government payments to the Queen. Payments will now be subject to scrutiny like any other government department expenditure, with adjustments for annual inflation.

Monday Dec 1 — **"Metric Speed-Up"** The Government is planning legislation to speed up the changeover to the metric programme, which is now well behind its original target date. It wants 'cut-off' dates to be imposed, after which the old imperial system cannot be used.

Tuesday 2 — **"Aerosol Report"** The Government plans to publish a report on possible dangers from the propellants used in aerosol sprays. Scientists at the Atomic Energy Research in Harwell are currently researching chlorofluorocarbons, which are the main ingredients.

HERE IN BRITAIN
"Future Transport"

London Transport's prototype double-deck bus for the 1980s has been unveiled. It has driver-controlled doors, which despite being more costly, will be safer.

The floor has been lowered by seven inches, making it easier for the elderly and infirm to step on board and giving tall people more head room and the engine is in a sound-proofed compartment at the back, so noise has been reduced. A new suspension system, power-assisted steering and hydraulic brakes give a very smooth ride, which indeed it ought to be at about £25,000 a vehicle.

AROUND THE WORLD
"Pacifist Gardener"

Philip Berrigan, a Catholic priest and peace activist, was arrested again for digging up the White House lawn in protest against American militarism and police brutality.

Known for his radical activism, Berrigan married a former nun in 1973 and was excommunicated by the Catholic Church.

Previously, he was arrested outside the British Embassy for spray-painting *'disarm or dig graves'* on the pavement and on Winston Churchill's statue. The embassy did not press charges, and Berrigan later entered White House grounds with other tourists.

Stir Up Sunday

'Stir-up Sunday' is a centuries old tradition, where on the last Sunday before Advent, housewives start 'stirring up' their Christmas puddings. It is a family affair, and even children are allowed to help weigh out and mix all the ingredients ready for steaming the pudding. Everyone is expected to take a turn to stir the pudding mix, for each person can make a special wish for the year ahead. Traditionally, the pudding should be stirred from east to west, in honour of the Wise Men who travelled from the East to visit the baby Jesus.

Rich Christmas puddings and fruit cakes benefit from being made this much in advance because it allows the flavours to intensify, and the colour deepen over time. Puddings can be re-steamed each week and many people will also 'feed' their cakes by pricking the base and pouring an eggcup full of brandy or rum over it, before wrapping it up again carefully to preserve the moisture. By Christmas, a good cake or pudding will be 'black and rotten' – very rich indeed!

The Christmas pudding originated in the 14th-century as a sort of porridge, originally known as 'frumenty', which bore little resemblance to the pudding we know today but, in the 17th century, changes to the recipe were made. It was thickened with eggs, breadcrumbs, dried fruit and beer or spirits were added – and it came to resemble something a bit more like a sweet pudding. Nowadays, the ingredients include raisins, currants, suet, brown sugar, breadcrumbs, carrot, mixed peel, flour, mixed spices, eggs, milk and brandy, which are all essential for keeping qualities. Puddings were traditionally boiled in a 'pudding cloth', although today are usually steamed in a basin, then brought to the table with a sprig of holly, doused in brandy and set alight.

Dec 3rd - Dec 9th 1975

IN THE NEWS

Wednesday 3 — **"Kirby Disaster Area"** A police report on Kirkby, Merseyside, calls for investment to address economic decline, crime, and planning errors. It praises local efforts, but highlights government neglect and inadequate infrastructure.

Thursday 4 — **"Herring Banned"** Herring fishing in the North Sea has been banned for a month, due to over fishing by other countries. The Federation of Fishmongers said, *"We do not envisage this increasing prices... there is currently a great shortage of herring...they simply are not there ... the decline in the last 15 years had been dramatic."*

Friday 5 — **"107 Schools Go Independent"** At least 107 of the 173 direct-grant grammar schools in England and Wales have decided to become independent rather than co-operate in the comprehensive education schemes.

Saturday 6 — **"Balcombe Street Siege"** One of four gunmen still barricaded with two hostages in a flat in London, is believed to be a man named by Scotland Yard as Michael Wilson, who is wanted in connection with the recent murder of Ross McWhirter.

Sunday 7 — **"Turtles in Space"** The Russians have sent turtles and plants to their Salyut space station on an unmanned Soyuz mission, to help in designing new life support systems for future cosmonauts.

Monday 8 — **"Saving Marriages"** Three Lancashire women have established Britain's first 'Family Crisis Centre', whose object is to help mend broken marriages and aid battered wives. They claim to have successfully saved seven marriages since setting up.

Tuesday 9 — **"Radiation leak"** Two airline workers were taken to hospital when an empty radioactive container was found to be leaking in a warehouse at Heathrow Airport, London, it has been revealed. The workers were allowed to go home after tests.

HERE IN BRITAIN
"Laddo The Lion"

Laddo's owner is ready to defy a West Midland's court ruling forbidding him to keep a lion at his home in Cradley Heath. He appeared in court with a lion tamer, who lives at the same address.
They were charged with behaving in a manner likely to cause a breach of the peace, by taking a wild animal for a tour around Birmingham. The case was adjourned for nine days. The accused commented, *"I am taking my lion out and I do not care if I get arrested and put in jail. He needs exercise badly."*

AROUND THE WORLD
"History Made by Orphans"

Historical figures were often orphans, abandoned or illegitimate children, a study of over 300 political and religious leaders reveals.

The list includes Lloyd George, Ivan the Terrible, and Queen Victoria, who lost their fathers before the age of eight, Attila, Ataturk, Lenin, Stalin, Hitler, who were orphaned before the age of 15. Calvin, Churchill, Martin Luther, Mao Tse-tung, Nasser, ex-President Nixon, President Tito and Mrs Golda Meir are examples of those rejected by their fathers or abandoned.

Letters To Santa

Children are swept up by the magic of Christmas, mostly with the anticipation of a visit from Father Christmas himself. In the past, local newspapers often used to publish original letters to him during the month of December and on Christmas Eve in 1928, the Dundee Evening Telegraph published a series of letters from local children.

'Dear Santa Claus, I wish you a Merry Xmas and a happy new year. Please will you give me a flash-lamp, a pencil box and a game of snakes and ladders and a cake of rubber and a pencil holder and please will you give me a ribbon for my cat and I would like you to give me an orange and an apple,' wrote one optimistic child.

'Dear Santa Claus, I would like a red waterproof coat and hat to keep the rain out of my clothes. I want six handkerchiefs for Sundays and a box of chocolates to eat,' wrote another.

The earliest known letter to him from the UK was written in 1895 by a young girl in Lincolnshire. The letter was addressed to 'Father Christmas, The North Pole, the GPO' and asked for a paint set. In the days of coal fires, the letters were often 'sent up the chimney', but now we have more electric fires and central heating, this isn't always possible and many letters are still posted, where despite the increased volume of mail at Christmas, the Post Office still provide a postal address for Father Christmas - c/o a PO Box in Lapland, and guarantee that if a letter to him is accompanied by a stamped addressed envelope, each child will get a reply. However, while this tradition has remained largely unchanged, the nature of the gifts requested *and expected* by children has changed dramatically!

Dec 10th - Dec 16th 1975

IN THE NEWS

Wednesday 10   **"Bigger Cars Please"** In a survey carried out by BP, despite the increases in costs, motorists still want to trade up to a bigger car, with half of trade-ups this year being to two-litre engines.

Thursday 11   **"Another Cod War"** The first shots of this latest cod war were fired from the Icelandic gunboat Thor, across the bows of two British support ships. Both ships collided with the Thor, causing extensive damage to the gunboat.

Friday 12   **"Christmas Cheese Ceremony"** The annual Christmas Cheeses ceremony dating back to 1692 was held at the Royal Hospital, in Chelsea, where a large wheel of cheese is blessed and cut with a sword, by one of the red-coated pensioners.

Saturday 13   **"Picasso's Heirs Inherit £650m"** Picasso's fortune included two chateaux, two Provence estates, bank accounts and dozens of sketches. The drawings, paintings and sculptures are deposited in the safes of several banks.

Sunday 14   **"Fog Affects Flights and Roads"** Roads and air services were badly disrupted by ice and fog, described by the RAC as the worst since the London "smogs" of the 1950s, with visibility as low as a yard in Kent.

Monday 15   **"Village Stores"** Nine men from Riseley, near Bedford were charged with handling and receiving stolen goods. The village was a distribution centre for stolen goods from universities, hospitals, colleges, private homes and a transport company.

Tuesday 16   **"First Female QC"** Judge Patricia Coles has become the first woman of Lincoln's Inn to be made a QC after being sworn in as a circuit judge by the Lord Chancellor at the House of Lords.

HERE IN BRITAIN

"Everett v Queen!"

A man, paying higher rates on his four-bedroom house than the Queen pays for an eight-bedroom farmhouse nearby, has appealed to West Norfolk Valuation Court. He also pays a £20 rating on his swimming pool, while the Duke of Kent's pool, also on the royal estate, is not rated.

The Queen's 'Wood Farm' has a total rate of £228.52, while Mr. Everett's house, commands £238.54. The court upheld Mr. Everett's assessment, deeming it fair, and said they would investigate the Duke's pool.

AROUND THE WORLD

"Fiji Island Paradise"

The American Theatre Film Corporation of Los Angeles wanted to film a thrilling event similar to that described in Peter Benchley's novel 'Jaws' and they chose the tropical island of Fiji for the location.

The event was to be a fight to the death between an experienced Australian diver and a 17' killer shark.

However, the fight, which would have netted the diver a fee of $1m, has been banned by the Fiji Government, as they objected to their island paradise being made the site for a blood sport.

HE'S BEHIND YOU!
THE CHRISTMAS PANTOMIME

This year's pantomime season at the Bradford Alhambra Theatre will open with Jack and the Beanstalk, starring popular comedian Charlie Drake. Once described as a "quaint, troubled, sympathetic little man strangely reminiscent of an ageing Botticelli cherub", Charlie Drake has endeared himself to audiences all over the country, with his catchphrase "Hello My Darlings". London-born, Charlie has battled his way through variety theatres and touring shows, into television, falling off roofs, through windows and into the nation's heart for the past 22 years.

The origins of pantomime date back to the 16th Century, where evidence of stock characters of a similar vein to modern day pantomimes could be found in Italian theatres. By the 18th Century, this had migrated to London's stages, where early pantomimes told classical stories using the original Italian stock characters. The Harlequin became the star of London pantomime, and the first Harlequin, John Rich, used his fortune to construct the Covent Garden Theatre, now a prominent feature of the London theatre scene. 'Harlequinades' - love stories full of slapstick humour and mimed to music, dominated the pantomime for over 100 years, until the Drury Lane Theatre implemented a speaking Harlequin and started writing pantomimes based on old English folk stories. Dick Whittington, Robin Hood and Babes in The Wood became household stories through theatre, and soon domestic culture and satire became a key theme of the pantomime, attracting enthusiastic audiences. The Victorian Pantomime, as this became known, changed the industry forever. Gone were mimes and classic stories, in favour of satire and slapstick, with the retention of a now stock character of a women authority figure played by a man.

Dec 17th - Dec 23rd 1975

IN THE NEWS

Wednesday 17   **"Smelly Dispute"** 21 workers at the Leyland Triumph car plant in Speke went on strike complaining about the smell from stray cats. 600 men stopped work while cleaners spent 45 minutes scrubbing the floor, after which the men protested that the floor was still wet and dangerous to work on.

Thursday 18   **"Unborn Child's Rights"** The Labour MP for Birmingham is to introduce a private member's Bill providing for rights in law for the unborn child, seeking damages if it should be born with deformities caused by drugs, nuclear or industrial waste.

Friday 19   **"Sappers Save Toads"** The Royal Engineers have dug a large pond on ranges at Longmoor Camp, Hampshire, so that the natter jack toad can be saved from extinction in southern England.

Saturday 20   **"Nuclear Waste Train Derailed"** A train loaded with used irradiated nuclear fuel from Japan was derailed at Barrow, a few hours after the cargo had arrived by sea for re-processing at Windscale, in Cumbria.

Sunday 21   **"Hepworth Museum"** A museum is to be opened in her former studio at St Ives, Cornwall, to form a permanent memorial to Dame Barbara Hepworth, the sculptor,

Monday 22   **"Babies Die of Cold"** According to Child Poverty Action Group, more than a thousand fewer babies would die in most years in Britain if they were sufficiently protected from the cold in their homes. It has been shown by several other countries that these seasonal deaths of babies can be completely prevented.

Tuesday 23   **"Festive Spirits"** A riding instructor, taking Christmas spirits too literally, pleaded guilty at Bow Street Magistrates' Court to being drunk in charge of a horse in Hyde Park.

HERE IN BRITAIN

"Plucking Rules"

A new EEC directive says that in future, plucking must be done in special processing sheds and not on individual turkey farms and the sale of fresh 'turkeys containing entrails must cease'.

The National Farmers' Union said it was giving freshly plucked turkeys to as many MPs as possible. *'We are not trying to bribe them, just trying to bring this situation to their notice.'* The threat of the directive has brought a cutback of a million fresh turkeys already this year amid fears that fresh turkey will virtually disappear from our Christmas menu.

AROUND THE WORLD

"Snail Poachers"

The authorities in the Swiss canton of Valais, in the South-West of the country, have placed a ban on the collection of Helix Pomatia or edible snails for the next three years in order to save the species from extinction.
They decided that *'the systematic collection of tons of snails over the past few years has endangered the species.'* Police and forest wardens have been empowered to search suspected poachers' bags for the snails, also known as Roman or Burgundy Snails, and if found guilty, they will face steep fines or a prison sentence.

The Trafalgar Tree

Norway's annual gift of a Christmas tree is in pride of place at Trafalgar Square, although the original excitement over the tree and its lights has somewhat dimmed over the years. The Acton Gazette led with the spartan headline, *'The traditional lighting-up of the Trafalgar Square Christmas tree is taking place tomorrow,'* and one gentleman due to retire commented, *'Tree? Who cares?'*

The first tree was sent from Oslo in 1947 as a token of gratitude to the British people for their help during the second world war when Great Britain was Norway's closest ally. London was where the Norwegian King Haakon VII and his government fled as their country was occupied, and it was from here that much of Norway's resistance movement was organised. Both the BBC and its Norwegian counterpart NRK would broadcast in Norwegian from London, something that was both an important source of information and a boost of morale for those who remained in Norway, where people would listen in secret to their forbidden radios. The idea to send a pine to Britain was first conceived by the Norwegian naval commando, Mons Urangsvå, who sent a tree from the island of Hisøy which had been cut down during a raid to London in 1942 as a gift to King Haakon and King George V decided that it should be installed in Trafalgar Square where it stood *'evergreen with defiant hope'*.

The trees come from the snow-covered forest area surrounding Oslo, known as "Oslomarka", an area populated with moose, lynx, roe deer, and even the odd wolf, and legions of pine trees. A worthy tree is located by the head forester and space is cleared around it to allow light from all angles, and it is tended through the years to secure optimal growth.

Dec 24th – Dec 31st 1975

IN THE NEWS

Wednesday 24 — **"All At Sea"** Light keeper Donald McLeod has left Stromness, Orkney, to spend a month on Sule Skerry, 30 miles west of Orkney in the Atlantic, Britain's most distant lighthouse.

Thursday 25 — **"Royals on Holiday"** The Queen's family will stay in the eight-bedroom Wood Farm, Sandringham, after Christmas, but Christmas Day will be spent at Windsor.

Friday 26 — **"Family Time"** A consultant geriatrician at a Battersea hospital, took seven members of his family to work with him, so they could celebrate Christmas Day together. Because of the junior doctors' dispute, he is working an 80-hour week.

Saturday 27 — **"Salvation Army"** Up to 2,200 of London's down-and-outs enjoyed some Christmas cheer at Salvation Army hostels where there were free meals, including a full turkey lunch.

Sunday 28 — **"Cold Feet"** Marie Mao, a French nun, was caught shoplifting in a West End store, and fined £35. Mlle Mao admitted stealing two pairs of socks worth £1.41.

Monday 29 — **"Equal Advertising"** Sex discrimination in advertising is now banned and adverts *'showing women at domestic tasks in the course of trying to sell people household items'* is being discouraged.

Tuesday 30 — **"Heat Saving Homes"** An important step in energy conservation has been taken by the Government to build a solar energy house, a heat reclaim house, and a heat pump house, which will use only two thirds of the heat of the average modern dwelling.

Wednesday 31 — **"No Women at The Bar"** On the day the Sex Discrimination Act came into force 'El Vino', the Fleet Street wine bar, adamantly refused to change the establishment's 96-year old tradition of not serving women at the bar.

HERE IN BRITAIN

"Mucky Love Letters"

Sir John French's indiscreet love letters to his mistress, while he was Commander-in-Chief of the British Expeditionary Force in Flanders, have been bought for £5,280 by the Imperial War Museum. French's granddaughter described the sale as *'the lowest form of muckraking'* and it was cashing in on a private affair of an intimate nature.

On the other hand, the granddaughter of French's *mistress* and vendor of the letters, replied, *'French has been dead 50 years. I feel that after this length of time these matters need not remain secret anymore.'*

AROUND THE WORLD

"Outsourcing Kidnap Insurance"

Despite Italian government opposition, the sale of insurance policies against the mounting wave of kidnappings is a flourishing form of business in these times of recession.

With Italian companies unable to engage openly in this, most business is channelled through London, but the Italian government has told insurance companies that this is bad practice and will promote further kidnappings - plus any insurance placed abroad adds to the outflow of Lira funds. No-one admits to being involved but many say, *'Kidnapping is a field which shows every prospect of further expansion'.*

GHOSTS AND GHOULS

The British fascination with ghostly tales around Christmas time goes back thousands of years and is rooted in ancient celebrations of the winter solstice. In the depths of winter, pagan traditions included a belief in a ghostly procession of riders across the sky, known as The Wild Hunt. Recounting stories of heroism against monstrous and supernatural beings became a midwinter tradition, with dark tales used to entertain on dark nights. Ghosts have been associated with winter cold ever since those ancient times, the 'Ode of Beowulf' being one of the oldest ghost stories, from about the 8th century, about a Scandinavian prince who fights the evil and terrifying monster Grendel. In 1611, Shakespeare wrote 'The Winter's Tale' which includes the line: *"A sad tale's best for winter, I have one of sprites and goblins."*

Almost 200 years later, Mary Shelley set her horror novel 'Frankenstein' in a snowy wasteland. The Victorians made the winter ghost story their own, with the idea of something dreadful lurking beyond the light and laughter, inspiring some famous chilling tales. Elizabeth Gaskell's 'The Old Nurse's Story', Wilkie Collin's 'The Haunted Hotel' and of course the classic Christmas tale of hauntings by Charles Dickens, 'A Christmas Carol' are some of the better-known titles from this period. Many traditional ghost stories are introduced using the literary device of a group of friends telling stories around a roaring fire rather like pagan storytellers around the midwinter fire. Now times have changed, and the central heating has replaced the roaring fire, but we still have a fear of the unknown, a yearning for what is lost and a desire to be secure, and paradoxically we still enjoy the jolt of fear and dread such stories convey, that make the Christmas lights glitter even more brightly.

1975 Calendar

January						
Su	Mo	Tu	We	Th	Fr	Sa
			1	2	3	4
5	6	7	8	9	10	11
12	13	14	15	16	17	18
19	20	21	22	23	24	25
26	27	28	29	30	31	

February						
Su	Mo	Tu	We	Th	Fr	Sa
						1
2	3	4	5	6	7	8
9	10	11	12	13	14	15
16	17	18	19	20	21	22
23	24	25	26	27	28	

March						
Su	Mo	Tu	We	Th	Fr	Sa
						1
2	3	4	5	6	7	8
9	10	11	12	13	14	15
16	17	18	19	20	21	22
23	24	25	26	27	28	29
30	31					

April						
Su	Mo	Tu	We	Th	Fr	Sa
		1	2	3	4	5
6	7	8	9	10	11	12
13	14	15	16	17	18	19
20	21	22	23	24	25	26
27	28	29	30			

May						
Su	Mo	Tu	We	Th	Fr	Sa
				1	2	3
4	5	6	7	8	9	10
11	12	13	14	15	16	17
18	19	20	21	22	23	24
25	26	27	28	29	30	31

June						
Su	Mo	Tu	We	Th	Fr	Sa
1	2	3	4	5	6	7
8	9	10	11	12	13	14
15	16	17	18	19	20	21
22	23	24	25	26	27	28
29	30					

July						
Su	Mo	Tu	We	Th	Fr	Sa
		1	2	3	4	5
6	7	8	9	10	11	12
13	14	15	16	17	18	19
20	21	22	23	24	25	26
27	28	29	30	31		

August						
Su	Mo	Tu	We	Th	Fr	Sa
					1	2
3	4	5	6	7	8	9
10	11	12	13	14	15	16
17	18	19	20	21	22	23
24	25	26	27	28	29	30
31						

September						
Su	Mo	Tu	We	Th	Fr	Sa
	1	2	3	4	5	6
7	8	9	10	11	12	13
14	15	16	17	18	19	20
21	22	23	24	25	26	27
28	29	30				

October						
Su	Mo	Tu	We	Th	Fr	Sa
			1	2	3	4
5	6	7	8	9	10	11
12	13	14	15	16	17	18
19	20	21	22	23	24	25
26	27	28	29	30	31	

November						
Su	Mo	Tu	We	Th	Fr	Sa
						1
2	3	4	5	6	7	8
9	10	11	12	13	14	15
16	17	18	19	20	21	22
23	24	25	26	27	28	29
30						

December						
Su	Mo	Tu	We	Th	Fr	Sa
	1	2	3	4	5	6
7	8	9	10	11	12	13
14	15	16	17	18	19	20
21	22	23	24	25	26	27
28	29	30	31			

IF YOU ENJOYED THIS BOOK PLEASE LEAVE A RATING OR REVIEW AT AMAZON

We have books for people born in almost all years between 1940 and 1980.

To see the full range scan the QR code and be taken to the Amazon page showing them all.

We also have framed prints to celebrate the year of your birth.
These make stylish and interesting gifts for birthdays, wedding anniversaries and other special times.
Each can be personalised with the recipient's name(s).

Scan the QR code to go directly to the framed prints.

Printed in Great Britain
by Amazon

95ea4483-fc1c-4ef6-b129-f1e3c76a4f9cR01